ROCK RECORDS · VOL. 2

THE ILLUSTRATED BOOK OF

ROCK

RECORDS

A DELILAH BOOK

Distributed by the
Putnam Publishing Group

volume 2

A Delilah Book
Delilah Communications, Ltd.
118 East 25th Street
New York, N.Y. 10010

Copyright © 1983 by Virgin Books

ISBN 0-933328-75-3
Library of Congress Catalog Card Number: 81: 71236

First published in the United States of America
by Delilah Communications, Ltd. in 1983

Originally published in Great Britain by
Virgin Books in 1983.

THE COMPILERS

Barry Lazell and Dafydd Rees are directors of the Media Research and Information Bureau (MRIB), a company which provides a variety of research and creative services to the publishing, music, broadcasting and other media industries. Their 'Rock Records: A Book of Lists', 'The Illustrated Book of Film Lists' and 'Chartfile Volume 1' and 'Chartfile Volume 2' (compiled with Alan Jones) have already been published by Virgin Books, and other titles are in preparation.

MRIB's work can also be found regularly in such journals as Sounds, No. 1, Kerrang, ZigZag, The Sun, Daily Star, Soundmaker, Video Trade Weekly, More Music, Video Business, Music Week and Record Mirror. The origination and co-ordination of the Marathon Music Quiz, broadcast by Radio 1 in 1982 and 1983, was also provided by MRIB.

The Lazell/Rees partnership was formed when both were founder members of the Record Business Research Department. Dafydd, resident in London, now directs operations from the company's Duke Street offices; Barry divides his time between his desk in the West End and his typewriter in mid-Essex.

WITH THANKS

Once again the compilers would like to thank several people without whose efforts this book would probably not be in your hands now: Luke and Maria at MRIB, Cat and John at Virgin, the Waldo's team for all their bits and pieces, Fred Dellar, the record company press officers who dug out photographs for us, and the myriad music papers and magazines whose ancient back issues provided source material for many of the lists in this second volume.

As in Volume One, charts and chart positions referred to in the text are in virtually all cases taken from reference to the compilers' own file of 'master charts', an amalgamated assessment of the individual charts published by Billboard and Cashbox in the USA, and by NME, Melody Maker, Disc, Music Week, Record Mirror and Record Business in the UK. We thank all these publications individually.

All photographs illustrating the book come from MRIB's own photo files, originating mainly from an assortment of British record companies. Memorabilia and printed matter reproduced in illustrations are also MRIB file items, gathered from a wide variety of original sources.

INTRODUCTION

There isn't a lot to say in introducing the Second Volume of **'Rock Records'** to be published by Virgin. We would like to thank the readers who eagerly devoured the fax 'n' trivia in Volume One, and effectively made it possible for us to serve up a second helping.

The emphasis in this book is slightly different — deliberately — as we felt we had exhausted most of the 'first' and 'best' categories in Volume One. We have gone instead for lots more esoteric and in many cases purely trivial lists, which we sincerely hope will fascinate and entertain readers as much as they did us during their compilation.

Reviewers in print and on radio and TV very obviously took the sillier parts of Volume One to Heart. On that basis, we should get a radio series out of this compilation, at least! (All enquiries from the media will be listened to sympathetically . . .)

That's it from us. Turn the page, get informed, and once again, have fun.

Barry and Dafydd, MRIB

A STAR IN THE LISTS★INDICATES ACCOMPANYING PHOTO

THE ACTS WHO SCORED IN THE UK SINGLES CHARTS FOR THE MOST CONSECUTIVE YEARS

1   ELVIS PRESLEY ★

28 years (1956-1983)

2   CLIFF RICHARD 17 years (1958-1974)★
3   ANDY WILLIAMS 15 years (1962-1976)
4 = HOT CHOCOLATE 14 years (1970-1983)
4 = DIANA ROSS 14 years (1970-1983)
6 = JIM REEVES 13 years (1960-1972)
6 = ELTON JOHN 13 years (1971-1983)
6 = ROD STEWART 13 years (1971-1983)
9 = DAVID BOWIE 12 years (1972-1983)
9 = HOLLIES 12 years (1963-1974)
9 = T.REX 12 years (1968-1977)
9 = FRANKIE VAUGHAN 12 years (1954-1965)
9 = STEVIE WONDER 12 years (1966-1977)
14 = FRANK SINATRA 11 years (1954-1964)
14 = STATUS QUO 11 years (1973-1983)
14 = SUPREMES 11 years (1964-1974)
17 = ABBA 10 years (1974-1983)
17 = MAX BYGRAVES 10 years (1952-1961)
17 = TOM JONES 10 years (1965-1974)
17 = ROY ORBISON 10 years (1960-1969)
17 = GENE PITNEY 10 years (1961-1970)

Just missing the top 20 are The Beatles, The Who, The Four Tops, Queen and Showaddywaddy, who all charted in nine consecutive years. Assuming Queen have a hit single during 1983, they could have joined the ranks at No.17 by the time you read this. It seems very likely too that Hot Chocolate, Diana Ross, Elton John, David Bowie, Status Quo, Rod Stewart and Abba will all be extending their runs.

Had Cliff Richard not had unaccountable blank years top 50-wise during 1975 and 1978, he would now have been running Elvis a very close second with 26 consecutive years of hits.

ROCK MOVIES OF THE 1950s (AND WHO WAS FEATURED IN THEM)

THE GIRL CAN'T HELP IT
(20th Century Fox, 1956)
EDDIE COCHRAN – 20 Flight Rock
FATS DOMINO – Blue Monday
GENE VINCENT – Be-Bop-A-Lula ★
JULIE LONDON – Cry Me A River
LITTLE RICHARD – The Girl Can't Help It/Ready Teddy/
    She's Got It
NINO TEMPO BAND – Tempo's Tempo
EDDIE FONTAINE – Cool It Baby
PLATTERS – You'll Never, Never Know
TRENIERS – Rockin' Is Our Business
JOHNNY OLEN – My Idea Of Love
RAY ANTHONY – Rock Around The Rockpile

GO JOHNNY GO *(Valiant, 1958)*
CHUCK BERRY – Little Queenie/Memphis Tennessee
EDDIE COCHRAN – Teenage Heaven
JIMMY CLANTON – Go Johnny Go/My Love Is True/
   A Ship On A Stormy Sea/Angel Face/It Takes A Long Time
JACKIE WILSON – You'd Better Know It
RITCHIE VALENS – Ooh My Head
JO-ANN CAMPBELL – Momma Can I Go Out?
FLAMINGOS – Jump Children
HARVEY FUQUA – Don't Be Afraid To Love Me
CADILLACS – Jaywalker/Please Mr Johnson
SANDY STEWART – Playmate/Heavenly Father/
   Once Again (with JIMMY CLANTON)

●

SHAKE, RATTLE AND ROCK
(American International, 1956)
FATS DOMINO – Ain't That A Shame/Honey Child/
   I'm In Love Again
JOE TURNER – Lipstick, Powder And Paint/Feelin' Happy
ANITA RAY – Rockin' Saturday Night
TOMMY CHARLES – Sweet Love On My Mind

●

THE BIG BEAT *(Universal, 1957)*
FATS DOMINO – The Big Beat/I'm Walkin'
DEL VIKINGS – Can't Wait
DIAMONDS – Little Darlin'/Where May Go, Go I

●

DISC JOCKEY JAMBOREE
(Warner Brothers, 1957)
JERRY LEE LEWIS – Great Balls Of Fire
CARL PERKINS – Glad All Over
FATS DOMINO – Wait And See
BUDDY KNOX – Hula Love
CHARLIE GRACIE – Cool Baby
JIMMY BOWEN – Cross Over
CONNIE FRANCIS – Sempre/For Children Of All Ages/
   Who Are We To Say (with PAUL CARR)/
   24 Hours A Day (with PAUL CARR)
FRANKIE AVALON – Teacher's Pet
FOUR COINS – A Broken Promise
LEWIS LYMON & THE TEENCHORDS – Your Last Chance
ANDY MARTIN – Record Hop Tonight

LET'S ROCK *(Columbia, 1958)*
DANNY & THE JUNIORS – At The Hop
ROY HAMILTON – Here Comes Love/Secret Path Of Love
PAUL ANKA – I'll Be Waiting There For You
ROYAL TEENS – Short Shorts
DELLA REESE – Lonelyville
TYRONES – Blast Off
JULIUS LaROSA – Crazy Party, Crazy/Perfect Strangers/
   Casual/There Are Times

●

UNTAMED YOUTH
(Warner Brothers, 1957)
EDDIE COCHRAN – Cotton Picker

●

HIGH SCHOOL CONFIDENTIAL
(MGM, 1958)
JERRY LEE LEWIS – High School Confidential ★

ROCK, ROCK, ROCK
(Warner Brothers, 1957)
FRANKIE LYMON & THE TEENAGERS – Baby Baby/
I'm Not A Juvenile Delinquent
JOHNNY BURNETTE ROCK'N'ROLL TRIO – Lonesome Train
CHUCK BERRY – You Can't Catch Me
FLAMINGOS – Would I Be Crying
JIMMY CAVELLO & THE HOUSEROCKERS –
Rock, Rock, Rock/The Big Beat
MOONGLOWS – Over And Over Again/I Knew From The Start
LAVERN BAKER – Tra La La
ALAN FREED & HIS BAND – Rock'n'Roll Boogie/
Right Now, Right Now
CONNIE FRANCIS (unseen "voice" of Tuesday Weld) –
I Never Had A Sweetheart/Little Blue Wren
BOWTIES – Ever Since I Can Remember/
Rock Pretty Baby (with IVY SHULMAN)
THREE CHUCKLES – Thanks To You/We're Gonna Rock Tonight/
The Things Your Heart Needs/Won't You Give Me A Chance?

●

DON'T KNOCK THE ROCK
(Columbia, 1956)
BILL HALEY & THE COMETS – Don't Knock The Rock/
Calling All Comets/Hot Dog Buddy Buddy/Hook, Line & Sinker
LITTLE RICHARD – Rip It Up/Tutti Frutti/Long Tall Sally
TRENIERS
DAVE APPELL & THE APPLEJACKS

●

JUKE BOX RHYTHM *(Columbia, 1959)*
JACK JONES – Juke Box Rhythm/The Freeze/Make Room For Joy
JOHNNY OTIS – Willie And The Hand Jive
EARL GRANT TRIO – I Feel It Right Here/Last Night
TRENIERS – Get Out Of The Car

●

ROCK, BABY, ROCK IT
(J.G. Tiger Films, 1957)
JOHNNY CARROLL & THE HOT ROCKS – Wild Wild Women/
Crazy Crazy Lovin'/Sugar Baby/Rockin' Maybelle
ROSCOE GORDON – Chicken In The Rough/Boppin'
CELL BLOCK SEVEN – Hot Rock/Rockin' Saints
PREACHER SMITH & THE DEACONS – Roogie Oogie/
Eat Your Heart Out
DON COATS & THE BON-AIRS – China Star/Love Never Forgets/
Stop The World
FIVE STARS – Funny Money/Love Is All I Need/Hey Juanita
BELEW TWINS – Lonesome/Love Me Baby

HOT ROD GANG
(Anglo Amalgamated, 1958)
GENE VINCENT & THE BLUE CAPS – Dance In The Street/
Baby Blue/Lovely Loretta/Dance To The Bop

●

ROCK AROUND THE CLOCK
(Columbia, 1955)
BILL HALEY & THE COMETS – Rock Around the Clock/
Razzle Dazzle/ABC Boogie/Mambo Rock/Rudy's Rock/
See You Later Alligator/Happy Baby/Rock-A-Beatin' Boogie/R.O.C.K.
FREDDY BELL & THE BELLBOYS – Giddy-Up-A-Ding-Dong/
We're Gonna Teach You To Rock
PLATTERS – The Great Pretender/Only You ★

CHUCK BERRY'S TEN FAVOURITE SINGLES – ALL HIS OWN!

During the early 1960s, the *New Musical Express* regularly ran a feature in which currently popular artists would list and comment on their all-time favourite ten singles. In the *NME* of May 29th, 1964, Chuck Berry appeared and chose ten of his own! As he explained: "Naturally I enjoy listening to other singers. But – and I hope I don't sound swollen-headed – my own recordings must be my favourites. You see, all my compositions come from my own experiences and all are commercial improvisations, so they mean more to me than any other discs." This was his list:

MAYBELLINE
My first record, which has now sold over two million copies. It was first taped on a cheap machine – sent 2,000 miles to California, 1,700 miles to New York City and then 300 miles to Chicago, where I re-recorded it and landed a contract with Chess Records. That was in May 1955, I was absolutely unknown. Two months later 'Maybelline' was in the US Top Ten.

SCHOOLDAYS
This is my second best seller and also my second favourite. I recorded it at a time when school-like songs were all the rage. And anyway, when I wrote it, I had very little experience of anything else but school to draw on.

SWEET LITTLE SIXTEEN
I wrote this one from travelling experiences on the road – as you know, a lot of towns are mentioned in the lyrics and I wrote bits of the song travelling along.

JOHNNY B. GOODE
My biographical experience came in handy again with this one.

MEMPHIS TENNESSEE
This has an especially warm place in my heart at the moment as it was the disc that put me back in the British charts after a long absence. I got my inspiration for this from a child in her mother's arms at one of my concerts in Memphis. She was melancholy among the joyous multitude and I built the story around this incident.

GO JOHNNY GO
This is really a sequel, or a continuation, of 'Johnny B. Goode'.

LET IT ROCK
I suppose I penned this about two years ago and it has in fact nothing to do with the advent of the rock era as I have heard many people say.

BACK IN THE USA
An imaginative story I penned as I was returning to America after a trip to Australia.

CAROL
I have only an imaginary girl in mind on this disc, but I believe I started to write it after playing at a dance.

ALMOST GROWN
This, like 'Schooldays', was taken from my boyhood experience.

THE RECORDS THE BEATLES RATED ON 'JUKE BOX JURY'

On December 7th, 1963, the BBC-TV pop panel programme *Juke Box Jury,* hosted by DJ David Jacobs, changed for once its usual policy of using a panel of four mixed musical or showbiz celebrities to rate the newly-released singles. The four members of the Beatles comprised the panel instead. This was the selection they heard, and how they rated them . . .

1 THE CHANTS — 'I Could Write A Book'
   All four raved over this choral vocal disc from a fellow Liverpool group whom they knew. They all voted it a hit, and chairman Jacobs asked rhetorically "Are they being too generous?"
   (Did not chart)

2 ELVIS PRESLEY — 'Kiss Me Quick'
   The general comment was that Elvis's voice was great but his material was scrappy in comparison with his earlier records. Nevertheless, all four voted it a hit.
   (Reached No. 14)

3 SWINGING BLUE JEANS — 'Hippy Hippy Shake'
   Ringo didn't like it as much as the Chan Romero original version, but George said it was a popular number around Liverpool already, and The Beatles used to do it themselves. All four rated it commercially; all voted it a hit.
   (Reached No. 2)

4 PAUL ANKA – 'Did You Have A Happy Birthday?'
George said he did, but that hearing this would put him off. The
others all disliked the song or the treatment, or both. All voted it a
miss.
(Did not chart)

5 SHIRLEY ELLIS – 'The Nitty Gritty'
This was shooting up the US charts at the time. All four said that
they liked it, and this style of record, a lot, but that it wouldn't be a
UK hit. "We haven't got around to that sort of thing yet", said
George. All four voted it a miss. David Jacobs thought it stood a good
chance, however, and asked the "second jury" (three audience
members) how they would vote on it. They made it a miss too.
(Did not chart)

6 STEVE LAWRENCE & EYDIE GORME –
'I Can't Stop Talking About You'
Paul and Ringo liked it; George admired the relaxed feel. John said it
sounded relaxed because "they're getting on a bit – I don't like it".
They voted it a hit by 3 to 1.
(Did not chart)

7 BILLY FURY – 'Do You Really Love Me Too'
Ringo said "not for me"; John and George tempered appreciation with reservations; Paul "quite liked it". They all recognised Fury's hit-making status, however, and all four voted it a hit.
(Reached No. 13)

8 BOBBY VINTON – 'There, I've Said It Again'
This was America's fastest-rising hit at the time. George thought it OK but not commercial, while John and Paul mused about the desirability of reviving old ballads. Ringo liked the smoothness: "Especially if you're sitting in one night, and not alone" – to which David Jacobs replied "Thank you, Don Juan Starr". All four voted it a miss.
(Reached No. 34)

9 THE ORCHIDS – 'Love Hit Me'
For John it was a straight poach of the Spector sound, though Paul thought this made it sound quite good for a British record. Ringo couldn't see it selling many, while George thought he'd rather have British groups pinch from the Crystals than other stuff. It was voted a miss by 3 to 1. The Orchids (three schoolgirls) were then introduced, having been secretly present. John thought that it was a dirty trick . . .
(Did not chart)

10 MERSEYBEATS – 'I Think Of You'
With time running short, there was no time for discussion of this one by another fellow Liverpudlian group. Asked to make a quick vote without comments, all four voted it a hit.
(Reached No. 5)

WHO WROTE THE LENNON/
McCARTNEY SONGS

Although every song John Lennon and Paul McCartney wrote during their Beatle years was credited to Lennon/McCartney by long-standing mutual agreement, it was always obvious that not every song could have been a straight 50/50 collaboration. In a special supplement in the UK music paper *Record Mirror* in October 1971, John Lennon went through the entire Lennon/McCartney songbook and identified which songs were his, which were Paul's, and which were true joint efforts. The following listings show how they broke down:

John Lennon songs

Please Please Me ("I was trying to do a Roy Orbison")
Do You Want To Know A Secret ("I wrote this for George")
I Call Your Name
Bad To Me
It Won't Be Long
I'm In Love
Hello Little Girl

I'll Be Back ("A nice tune, though the middle is a bit tatty")
I Feel Fine
No Reply
It's Only Love ("That's the one song I really hate of mine — terrible lyric")
Day Tripper
Norwegian Wood
What Goes On
In My Life
Run For Your Life ("Another one I never liked")
She Said, She Said
And Your Bird Can Sing ("Another horror")
Dr. Robert
Tomorrow Never Knows
Lucy In The Sky With Diamonds ("This was Julian's title; nothing to do with LSD")

Being For The Benefit Of Mr Kite ("I got some of the words off an old circus poster")
Good Morning, Good Morning
I Am The Walrus
Revolution
Happiness Is A Warm Gun
Julia
Sexy Sadie
Because
Across The Universe ("One of my best songs; I like the lyrics")

Everybody's Got Something To Hide Except Me and My Monkey
There's A Place
This Boy
All I've Got To Do
Not A Second Time
You Can't Do That
A Hard Day's Night
I Should Have Known Better
If I Fell
I'm Happy Just To Dance With You
Tell Me Why
Anytime At All
I'll Cry Instead
When I Get Home
I'm A Loser
I Don't Want To Spoil The Party
Ticket To Ride
Yes It Is
Help!
You've Got To Hide Your Love Away
You're Gonna Lose That Girl
Nowhere Man

Girl
Rain
I'm Only Sleeping
Strawberry Fields Forever
Dear Prudence
Glass Onion
The Continuing Story Of Bungalow Bill
I'm So Tired
Yer Blues
Cry Baby Cry
Goodnight
The Ballad Of John & Yoko
Come Together
I Want You (She's So Heavy)
Mean Mr. Mustard
Polythene Pam
One After 909
Hey Bulldog
Don't Let Me Down
You Know My Name (Look Up The Number)
Sun King
Dig A Pony
Dig It

Paul McCartney songs

Love Me Do
P.S. I Love You ("It was meant to be a Shirelles kind of song")
I'll Be On My Way

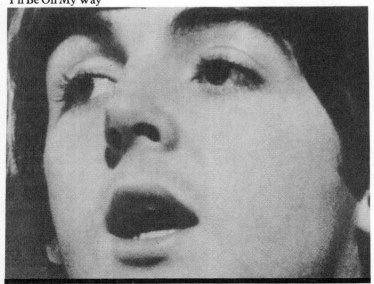

All My Loving
I'll Keep You Satisfied
Love Of The Loved
From A Window
Like Dreamers Do
A World Without Love
One And One Is Two ("That was a terrible one")
She's A Woman
I'll Follow The Sun
Yesterday ("Wow, that was a good 'un")
We Can Work It Out
Paperback Writer
Here, There And Everywhere
Good Day Sunshine
For No One ("Another of his I really liked")
Got To Get You Into My Life
Penny Lane
With A Little Help From My Friends
Getting Better
When I'm 64
Magical Mystery Tour
Hey Jude ("That's his best song. It started off as a song about my
    son Julian")
Back In The USSR
Rocky Raccoon
Why Don't We Do It In The Road ("One of his best")
I Saw Her Standing There
Tip Of My Tongue
Nobody I Know
Things We Said Today
I Don't Want To See You Again
I'm Down
The Night Before
Another Girl
Tell Me What You See
I've Just Seen A Face
That Means A Lot
You Won't See Me
I'm Looking Through You
Woman
Sgt. Pepper's Lonely Hearts Club Band
Fixing A Hole
Lovely Rita
Hello Goodbye
Your Mother Should Know
The Fool On The Hill
Step Inside Love
Ob-La-Di, Ob-La-Da
Martha My Dear

Blackbird
I Will
Mother Nature's Son
Helter Skelter
Honey Pie
Lady Madonna
All Together Now
Get Back
Let It Be
Maxwell's Silver Hammer
Oh Darling
You Never Give Me Your Money
She Came In Through The Bathroom Window
Golden Slumbers
Carry That Weight
The End
Her Majesty
Two Of Us On Our Way Home
The Long And Winding Road

Lennon-McCartney collaborations

From Me To You
Thank You Girl ("This was just a silly song we knocked off")
She Loves You ("We wrote it together on tour")
I'll Get You
I Want To Hold Your Hand
Baby's In Black
Misery ("This was mainly mine, though, I think")
Little Child
Hold Me Tight ("Mainly Paul")
I Wanna Be Your Man ("I helped him finish it")
Can't Buy Me Love
And I Love Her ("The first half was Paul's and the middle eight is mine")
Eight Days A Week ("We were trying to write the title song for 'Help',
    because there was at one time an idea of calling the film 'Eight Arms
    To Hold You', or something")
Michelle
Eleanor Rigby
Yellow Submarine ("Paul wrote the catchy chorus. I helped with the
    other blunderbuss bit")
She's Leaving Home
Drive My Car
Every Little Thing
What You're Doing
Baby You're A Rich Man ("We just stuck two songs together for
    this one")
Birthday
I've Got a Feeling
A Day In The Life ("I wrote the bit up to 'woke up, fell out of bed', and I
    think Paul wrote 'I'd love to turn you on'. I got the idea from a news
    item in the *Daily Mail* about 4000 holes in Blackburn")

THE BRITISH RECORD INDUSTRY BRITANNIA AWARDS

During 1977, the year which marked both the centenary of recorded sound and the Queen's Silver Jubilee, the UK record industry (co-ordinated by the BPI) presented a series of awards to mark excellence and achievement in British and international music and recording over the previous 25 years. It was originally intended to make the awards an annual "Oscar"-type celebration — but such plans appear to have been shelved indefinitely.

In Academy Award style, nominations and votes were taken in each category from BPI member companies, all the voting being on a one company-one vote basis, irrespective of size.

The awards were presented at a special dinner at Wembley Conference Centre on October 18th, 1977, and shown by Thames TV two days later to a television audience of almost 12 million viewers. Oddly, in very un-Oscar-like style, a fair number of nominees and winners failed to attend the event, though the on-stage performances by those who did attend — notably Simon & Garfunkel and Cliff Richard — provided the event with its highlights.

The rock and pop categories are listed below (there were also awards for the classical, spoken word and "service to industry" areas), and include all nominees as well as the winners.

BEST BRITISH POP SINGLE, 1952–1977
Joint winners: QUEEN ★
       — 'Bohemian Rhapsody'
       PROCOL HARUM
       — 'A Whiter
       Shade Of Pale'

Other nominees: BEATLES
       — 'She Loves You'
       10CC
       — 'I'm Not In Love'

BEST BRITISH POP ALBUM, 1952–1977
Winner: BEATLES – 'Sgt. Pepper's Lonely Hearts Club Band'
Other nominees: PINK FLOYD – 'The Dark Side Of The Moon'
ELTON JOHN – 'Goodbye Yellow Brick Road'
MIKE OLDFIELD – 'Tubular Bells'

BEST INTERNATIONAL POP SINGLE, 1952–1977
Winner: SIMON & GARFUNKEL – 'Bridge Over Troubled Water'
Other nominees: ELVIS PRESLEY – 'Jailhouse Rock'
FRANK SINATRA – 'My Way'
IKE & TINA TURNER – 'River Deep, Mountain High'

BEST INTERNATIONAL POP ALBUM, 1952–1977
Winner: SIMON & GARFUNKEL – 'Bridge Over Troubled Water'
Other nominees: ABBA – 'Arrival'
CAROLE KING – 'Tapestry'
STEVIE WONDER – 'Songs In The Key Of Life'

BEST BRITISH POP GROUP, 1952–1977
Winner: BEATLES
Other nominees: PINK FLOYD
ROLLING STONES
WHO

BEST BRITISH MALE SOLO ARTIST, 1952–1977
Winner: CLIFF RICHARD
Other nominees: Tom Jones
Elton John
Rod Stewart

BEST BRITISH FEMALE SOLO ARTIST, 1952–1977
Winner: SHIRLEY BASSEY
Other nominees: Petula Clark
Dusty Springfield
Cleo Laine

MOST OUTSTANDING NEW BRITISH RECORDING ARTIST
Joint winners: JULIE COVINGTON
GRAHAM PARKER
Other nominees: Bonnie Tyler
Heatwave

BEST BRITISH RECORD PRODUCER, 1952–1977
Winner: GEORGE MARTIN
Other nominees: Mickie Most
Gus Dudgeon
Glyn Johns

THE ACTS ON THE FIRST AND LAST "OH BOY" SHOWS

Jack Good's *Oh Boy* was the first almost entirely rock & roll orientated show on British TV, and it set the standard (rarely equalled) for all that followed. It was broadcast live from the stage of the Hackney Empire in London every Saturday on the 6 pm ITV slot, and ran from mid-June 1958 until the end of May the following year. The show can take a large share of the credit for breaking Cliff Richard (who first appeared during its third week, and in 19 shows thereafter) into a national star.

The acts on the first edition (June 15th, 1958) were:
MARTY WILDE
DALLAS BOYS
JOHN BARRY SEVEN
LORD ROCKINGHAM'S XI
CHERRY WAINER with RED PRICE
NEVILLE TAYLOR & THE CUTTERS
VERNON GIRLS
BERNICE READING
DUDLEY HESLOP
KERRY MARTIN

And on the final show
(May 30th, 1959):
CLIFF RICHARD
& THE DRIFTERS

MARTY WILDE
BILLY FURY
DICKIE PRIDE
DALLAS BOYS
CHERRY WAINER
DON LANG
RED PRICE
VERNON GIRLS
CUDDLY DUDLEY
MIKE PRESTON
PETER ELLIOTT
BILL FORBES
LORD ROCKINGHAM'S XI
NEVILLE TAYLOR & THE CUTTERS

Artists who guested on other shows during the series included Conway Twitty, Lonnie Donegan, Vince Eager, Tony Sheridan, Dickie Valentine, Shirley Bassey, Vince Taylor & The Playboys, Michael Holliday, The King Brothers, Chris Andrews, Ronnie Carroll, Jackie Dennis, Roy Young, and The Marino Marini Quartet.

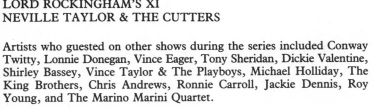

THE SHORTEST PERIOD OF TIME BETWEEN NO.1 HITS BY THE SAME ACT (UK CHARTS)

BEATLES — 'She Loves You' was replaced immediately by 'I Want To Hold Your Hand' (1963)★

JOHN LENNON — 'Imagine' was replaced immediately by 'Woman' (1981)

FRANKIE LAINE — one week between 'Hey Joe' and 'Answer Me' (1953)

BEATLES — one week between 'Get Back' and 'The Ballad Of John & Yoko' (1969)

JOHN LENNON — two weeks between '(Just Like) Starting Over' and 'Imagine' (1980/81)

ELVIS PRESLEY — three weeks between 'It's Now Or Never' and 'Are You Lonesome Tonight?' (1961)

ELVIS PRESLEY — three weeks between 'Are You Lonesome Tonight?' and 'Wooden Heart' (1961)

ELVIS PRESLEY — four weeks between 'Wooden Heart' and 'Surrender' (1961)

ROLLING STONES — six weeks between '(I Can't Get No) Satisfaction' and 'Get Off Of My Cloud' (1965)

BEATLES — six weeks between 'Paperback Writer' and 'Yellow Submarine'/'Eleanor Rigby' (1966)

JOHN TRAVOLTA & OLIVIA NEWTON-JOHN — six weeks between 'You're The One That I Want' and 'Summer Nights' (1978) ★

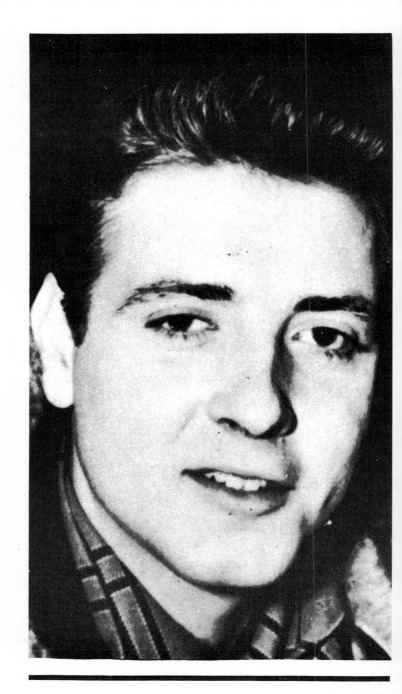

AMERICAN RECORDS WHICH REACHED NO.1 IN BRITAIN WITHOUT CHARTING IN THE US

THREE STEPS TO HEAVEN Eddie Cochran (1960)★
WOODEN HEART Elvis Presley (1961)
WHAT A WONDERFUL WORLD Louis Armstrong (1968)
I'LL NEVER FALL IN LOVE AGAIN Bobbie Gentry (1969)
WAND'RIN STAR Lee Marvin (1970)
DAYDREAMER/THE PUPPY SONG David Cassidy (1973)★
IF Telly Savalas (1975)
TEARS ON MY PILLOW Johnny Nash (1975)
I CAN'T GIVE YOU ANYTHING (BUT MY LOVE)
   Stylistics (1975)
WHEN A CHILD IS BORN (SOLEADO)
   Johnny Mathis (1976)
CHANSON D'AMOUR Manhattan Transfer (1977)
BRIGHT EYES Art Garfunkel (1979)
TOGETHER WE ARE BEAUTIFUL Fern Kinney (1980)
THEME FROM M*A*S*H M*A*S*H (1980)
USE IT UP AND WEAR IT OUT Odyssey (1980)

Some of these singles, like Presley's 'Wooden Heart', were not released in the US at the time of their British success. Others were novelties or film tie-ins which seemed to click with British tastes but were not, however, promoted in America.

WAITING LIMITED TO 10 MINS IN ANY HOUR

THE ALMOST ALL-BRITISH AMERICAN TOP TEN

During the week ending May 8th, 1965, the British invasion of American pop music reached its height: of the best-selling ten singles in the US, nine were of British origin. Not surprisingly, this achievement has never been equalled. Here's how the top ten looked:

1 (1) MRS BROWN YOU'VE GOT A LOVELY DAUGHTER
       Herman's Hermits (MGM)★
2 (7) COUNT ME IN Gary Lewis & The Playboys (Liberty)
3 (15) TICKET TO RIDE Beatles (Capitol)
4 (3) THE GAME OF LOVE
       Wayne Fontana & The Mindbenders (Fontana)
5 (2) I KNOW A PLACE Petula Clark (Warner Bros)
6 (6) I'LL NEVER FIND ANOTHER YOU Seekers (Capitol)
7 (9) SILHOUETTES Herman's Hermits (MGM)
8 (4) I'M TELLING YOU NOW Freddie & The Dreamers (Tower)★
9 (8) THE LAST TIME Rolling Stones (London)
10 (14) CAST YOUR FATE TO THE WIND
       Sounds Orchestral (Parkway)

No prizes for spotting the sole American record — Gary Lewis, the son of comedian Jerry, riding at No. 2 with the follow-up to his million-seller 'This Diamond Ring'. The next highest-placed American artist, at No. 11, was Marvin Gaye with 'I'll Be Doggone'.

THE FIRST ALL-BRITISH UK TOP TEN

On March 7th, 1964, well over a decade after singles charts were first introduced into Britain, the top ten sellers consisted for the first time ever of entirely domestic recordings by UK artists. In fact, the top 12 positions were all British, the highest-placed American act being Brenda Lee at No. 13 with 'As Usual', a record which had dropped from No. 9 the previous week. Below Brenda were six more Britons, and the only other American in the top 20 was Gene Pitney in the anchor position — ironically with a British song, 'That Girl Belongs To Yesterday', by Jagger & Richard.

These are the records which made up that historic top ten:

1 (1) ANYONE WHO HAD A HEART Cilla Black (Parlophone)
2 (4) BITS AND PIECES Dave Clark Five (Columbia)
3 (2) DIANE Bachelors (Decca)
4 (5) I THINK OF YOU Merseybeats (Fontana)
5 (3) NEEDLES AND PINS Searchers (Pye)
6 (13) NOT FADE AWAY Rolling Stones (Decca)
7 (30) LITTLE CHILDREN Billy J. Kramer & The Dakotas
       (Parlophone)
8 (6) I'M THE ONE Gerry &
       The Pacemakers (Columbia)★
9 (7) CANDY MAN Brian Poole
       & The Tremeloes (Decca)
10 (14) BOYS CRY Eden Kane
       (Fontana/Ritz)

The rest of the top 20 reads as follows:

11 (8) 5-4-3-2-1 Manfred Mann (HMV)
12 (16) OVER YOU Freddie & The Dreamers (Columbia)
13 (9) AS USUAL Brenda Lee (Brunswick)
14 (10) I'M THE LONELY ONE Cliff Richard (Columbia)
15 (18) STAY AWHILE Dusty Springfield (Philips)
16 (12) ALL MY LOVING (EP) Beatles (Parlophone)
17 (33) JUST ONE LOOK Hollies (Parlophone)
18 (11) HIPPY HIPPY SHAKE Swinging Blue Jeans (HMV)
19 (21) LET ME GO, LOVER Kathy Kirby (Decca)★
20 (34) THAT GIRL BELONGS TO YESTERDAY
       Gene Pitney (United Artists)

A week later, the top 12 records were still all British, although slightly reshuffled and with the Hollies' 'Just One Look' replacing the fading '5-4-3-2-1'. Gene Pitney was the highest-placed American at No. 13.

UK CHART ACTS WITH THE SHORTEST NAMES

M
U2
ABC
ACE
CAN
FOX
GAZ
GUN
★JAM
MAN
MUD
999
PhD
SHY
SKY
UFO ★
WAR
WHO
XTC
YES

Acts with full stops after each initial letter are not included, nor are Wah! because their exclamation mark counts as a letter.

SONGS WITH RED INDIAN CONNECTIONS

APACHE (Shadows)
INDIAN RESERVATION (Raiders)
RUNNING BEAR (Johnny Preston)
WIG WAM BAM (Sweet)
INDIAN LOVE CALL (Slim Whitman)
KEEM-O-SABE (Electric Indian)
GERONIMO (Shadows)
I'M AN INDIAN TOO
    (Don Armando's Second Avenue Rhumba Band
SOLDIER BLUE (Buffy Saint-Marie)
WITCH QUEEN OF NEW ORLEANS (Redbone)

The last two on the list are there because the acts concerned are of Red Indian descent (also, 'Soldier Blue' was the theme to a film about white/ Indian relations). Electric Indian, which hit in 1969, was interesting in being a studio instrumental outfit put together by Len (1-2-3) Barry.

ACTS WHO SHARE THEIR NAME WITH THE TITLE OF SOMEONE ELSE'S HIT RECORD

We are not suggesting that the matches are anything but coincidental, but there have been quite a few hit-makers through the years whose names have been exactly the same as titles of songs made into hits by somebody else. Here's a selection . . .

ABC (a hit for the Jackson 5)
AMERICA (a hit for Simon & Garfunkel and for David Essex —
   different songs)
A TASTE OF HONEY (a hit for Herb Alpert's Tijuana Brass)
THE BEAT (a hit for The Rockin' R's)
CARS (a hit for Gary Numan)
CHICAGO (a hit for Frank Sinatra)
CO-CO (a hit for Sweet)
DAWN (a hit for The Four Seasons)
DEEP PURPLE (a hit for Nino Tempo & April Stevens)
DIAMONDS (a hit for Jet Harris & Tony Meehan)
EMOTIONS (a hit for Brenda Lee)
FREE (a hit for Deniece Williams)
GALAXY (a hit for War)
GUESS WHO (a hit for Jesse Belvin)
HEART (a hit for Max Bygraves and for Rita Pavone —
   different songs)
HEATWAVE (a hit for Martha & The Vandellas)
★ IMAGINATION (a hit for Rocky Sharpe and The Replays) ★

JIMMY JONES (a hit for The Vapors — though spelled 'Jimmie Jones')
KISS (a hit for Dean Martin)
KOKOMO (a hit for Gene & Eunice)
LOVE (a hit for John Lennon)
MATCHBOX (a hit for Carl Perkins)
NEW YORK CITY (a hit for T. Rex)
RAINBOW (a hit for Marmalade and for Russ Hamilton —
    different songs)
RAINDROPS (a hit for Dee Clark)
SAILOR (a hit for Petula Clark)
SHEILA (a hit for Tommy Roe)
SUNNY (a hit for Bobby Hebb, Georgie Fame and Cher)
SWEET DREAMS (a hit for Roy Buchanan and for Tommy McLain)
SWEET SENSATION (a hit for The Melodians)
TRACIE (a hit for The Cuff Links — though spelled 'Tracy')
WAR (a hit for Edwin Starr)
WHAM! (a hit for Lonnie Mack)
YES (a hit for Ben E. King)

Stretching the point a little, there have also been some borderline cases, like 'Pretty Thing', 'Applejack', 'Moody Blue', 'Rolling Stone', 'Honeycomb', and 'Teddy Bear'.

BOTTOM OF THE LEAGUE

A rare collection of artists whose only American pop chart success was to fill the No. 100 slot in the top 100 singles chart for just one week. This, of course, still represents considerably more success than that achieved by the thousands of acts who have never attained any chart, anywhere . . .

SWALLOWS — 'Itchy Twitchy Feeling' (1958)
LEE AND PAUL — 'The Chick' (1959)
JIMMIE BEAUMONT — 'Ev'rybody's Cryin'' (1961)
TEXANS — 'Green Grass Of Texas' (1961)
HELEN SHAPIRO — 'Walkin' Back To Happiness' (1961)
EXCELS — 'Can't Help Lovin' That Girl Of Mine' (1961)
PETE ANTELL — 'Nite Time' (1962)
CARROLL BROTHERS — 'Sweet Georgia Brown' (1962)
STOMPERS — 'Quarter To Four Stomp' (1962)
CASTLE SISTERS — 'Goodbye Dad' (1962)
CHARMETTES — 'Please Don't Kiss Me Again' (1963)
MONITORS — 'Greetings (This Is Uncle Sam)' (1966)
VONTASTICS — 'Day Tripper' (1966)
A.B. SKHY — 'Camel Back' (1969)
BRIAN AUGER & THE TRINITY — 'Listen Here' (1970)
PETER YARROW — 'Don't Ever Take Away My Freedom' (1972) ★
FIRE AND RAIN — 'Hello Stranger' (1973)
21ST CENTURY — 'Remember The Rain' (1975)
DEBBIE TAYLOR — 'I Don't Wanna Leave You' (1976)
DANNY WHITE — 'Dance Little Lady, Dance' (1977)
PHILHARMONICS — 'For Elise' (1977)
LOVERS — 'Discomania' (1977)

One or two of these artists also found fame elsewhere, however — Peter Yarrow, for instance, was originally one third of Peter, Paul & Mary, while Helen Shapiro, the only British artist on the list, scored much better at home with 'Walkin' Back To Happiness', taking it to No. 1.

REAL-LIFE WOMEN WHO HAVE HAD SONGS WRITTEN ABOUT THEM

PATTIE BOYD ★
'Layla' — Derek & The Dominoes
JENNY BOYD
'Jennifer Juniper' — Donovan
PATTI D'ARBANVILLE
'Lady D'Arbanville' — Cat Stevens
LINDA EASTMAN
'Linda' — Jan & Dean
NANCY SINATRA
'Nancy (With The Laughing Face)' — Frank Sinatra
RITA COOLIDGE
'Delta Lady' — Joe Cocker
CAROLE KING
'Oh Carol' — Neil Sedaka
ANGIE BOWIE
'Angie' — Rolling Stones
PEGGY SUE GERROW
'Peggy Sue' — Buddy Holly (she actually married
   Jerry "J.I." Allison, Holly's friend and drummer)
SARA LOWNDS
'Sad-Eyed Lady Of The Lowlands' — Bob Dylan ★
   (Sara was Dylan's wife)

Pattie and Jenny Boyd must be the only two sisters in the world to have hit songs written about each of them by different artists. Jan & Dean's 'Linda' in 1963 was actually a revival; the song was originally written about Linda Eastman in 1947, when she was a little girl. She was the daughter of Lee Eastman, lawyer and friend to the songwriter, Jack Lawrence.

... AND REAL-LIFE MEN WHO HAVE HAD SONGS WRITTEN ABOUT THEM

DON McLEAN
'Killing Me Softly With His Song' — Roberta Flack
SYD BARRETT ★
'Shine On You Crazy Diamond' — Pink Floyd
BUDDY HOLLY
'Old Friend' — Waylon Jennings
JIMI HENDRIX
'Song For A Dreamer' — Procol Harum
BOB DYLAN
'Diamonds And Rust' — Joan Baez
WARREN BEATTY
'You're So Vain — Carly Simon
BRIAN EPSTEIN
'Baby You're A Rich Man' — Beatles
NEIL SEDAKA ★
'Oh Neil' — Carole King
PAUL McCARTNEY
'How Do You Sleep' — John Lennon
  (generally accepted to be about Paul)
VINCENT VAN GOGH
'Vincent' — Don McLean

'Oh Neil' was written by Carole King as a straight answer record to the song he'd just written about her ('Oh Carol'). Lori Leiberman originally recorded 'Killing Me Softly' after being captivated by McLean at one of his shows. And finally, if we accept that John Lennon's 'How Do You Sleep' is an indictment of Paul McCartney and his lifestyle, then McCartney's 'Let Me Roll It' on the *Band On The Run* album is definitely the answer record.

JOHN'S CHILDREN

Fan Club : c/o Gillian Ross,
65 Gaysham Hall,
Clayhall, Ilford, Essex.

Also the group's own club
"John's Children's"
22a Bridge St., Leatherhead, Surrey.
Discs Mon - Thur. Groups Fri - Sun.

GIRLS' NAMES WHICH BECAME SONG TITLES

There are hundreds of these. It seems that if you're stuck for inspiration for a song, you can always pick out a girl's name at random and write the rest of the lyric around it. To qualify for this list, the song title has to be just the name and nothing else — hence 'Anna (Go With Him)' and 'My Sharona', for instance, would not be eligible. From that point, we've selected 140 songs which were either hit singles or well-known recordings by the artists concerned.

1 ADRIENNE Tommy James
2 ALISON Elvis Costello
3 AMANDA Stuart Gillies
4 AMIE Pure Prairie League
5 ANASTASIA Pat Boone
6 ANDREA Sunrays
7 ANGIE Rolling Stones
8 ANNABELLA John Walker
9 BABETTE Tommy Bruce
10 BARBARA ANN Beach Boys★
11 BERNADETTE Four Tops
12 BETH Kiss
13 BILLIE JEAN Michael Jackson
14 BRANDY Scott English
15 BRENDA Cupids
16 CANDIDA Dawn
17 CANDY Astors
18 CAROL Chuck Berry
19 CAROLYN Merle Haggard
20 CAROLINE Status Quo
21 CARRIE Cliff Richard
22 CARRIE ANNE Hollies ★
23 CATERINA Perry Como
24 CECILIA Simon & Garfunkel
25 CHARMAINE Bachelors
26 CHRISTINE Siouxsie & The Banshees
27 CLAIR Gilber O'Sullivan
28 CLAIRE Paul & Barry Ryan
29 CLAUDETTE Everly Brothers
30 COLETTE Billy Fury
31 DAISY JANE America
32 DEBORA Tyrannosaurus Rex
33 DELILAH Tom Jones
34 DENISE Randy & The Rainbows
35 DESDEMONA John's Children ★
36 DIANA Paul Anka
37 DIANE Bachelors

38 DONNA Ritchie Valens
39 ELENORE Turtles
40 ELOISE Barry Ryan
41 ELVIRA Oak Ridge Boys
42 EMMA Hot Chocolate
43 EVE Jim Capaldi
44 FELICITY Orange Juice
45 FRANCENE Z.Z. Top
46 GAYE Clifford T. Ward
47 GIGI Billy Eckstine
48 GERALDINE Jack Scott
49 GINA Johnny Mathis
50 GLORIA Them
51 JACQUELINE Bobby Helms
52 JANE Jefferson Starship ★
53 JEAN Oliver
54 JEANETTE Beat
55 JEANNIE Danny Williams
56 JENNIFER Bobby Sherman
57 JENNIE LEE Jan & Arnie
58 JESSICA Allman Brothers Band
59 JESAMINE Casuals
60 JEZEBEL Frankie Laine
61 JILL Gary Lewis & The Playboys
62 JOANNE Michael Nesmith
63 JOANNA Scott Walker ★
64 JODY Del Shannon
65 JOLENE Dolly Parton
66 JOSIE Kris Kristofferson
67 JOSEPHINE Bill Black's Combe
68 JOY Mitch Ryder
69 JUDY Elvis Presley
70 JULIA Beatles
71 JULIE ANN Kenny
72 JULIET Four Pennies
73 JUSTINE Righteous Brothers
74 KATE Johnny Cash

75 KELLY Del Shannon ★
76 LANA Roy Orbison
77 LAYLA Derek & The Dominoes
78 LINDA Jan & Dean
79 LISA Jeanne Black
80 LOLA Kinks
81 LORELEI Lonnie Donegan
82 LORRAINE Bad Manners
83 LOUISE Phil Everly
84 LUANNE Foreigner
85 LYDIA Dean Friedman
86 MAGGIE Redbone

87 MANDY Barry Manilow
88 MARGIE Fats Domino
89 MARIA P.J. Proby
90 MARIANNE Cliff Richard
91 MARIE Bachelors
92 MARLENA Four Seasons

93 MARY LOU Ronnie Hawkins
94 MATILDA Cookie & The Cupcakes
95 MAYBELLINE Chuck Berry
96 MELISSA Allman Brothers Band
97 MICHELLE Beatles
98 MOLLY Bobby Goldsboro
99 NOLA Billy Williams
100 PATRICIA Perez Prado
101 PATSY Jack Scott
102 PATTI-ANN Johnny Crawford
103 PEGGY SUE Buddy Holly
104 PRISCILLA Eddie Cooley
105 RAMONA Bachelors
106 ROBERTA Barry & The Tamerlanes
107 RONNIE Four Seasons
108 ROSALIE Thin Lizzy
109 ROSALYN Pretty Things
110 ROSANNA Toto
111 ROSE MARIE Slim Whitman
112 ROSIE Don Partridge
113 ROXANNE Police
114 ROSETTA Alan Price & Georgie Fame
115 RUBY Ray Charles ★
116 RUBY ANN Marty Robbins
117 SADIE Detroit Spinners
118 SALLY Gerry Monroe
119 SALLY ANN Joe Brown
120 SAMANTHA Kenny Ball
121 SANDY John Travolta
122 SARA Fleetwood Mac
123 SARAH Thin Lizzy
124 SHEILA Tommy Roe
125 SHERRY Four Seasons
126 SHIRLEY Shakin' Stevens
127 SUSAN Buckinghams
128 SUZANNE Leonard Cohen
129 SYLVIA Focus
130 TAMMY Debbie Reynolds
131 TANSY Alex Welsh
132 TERESA Joe Dolan
133 TINA MARIE Perry Como
134 TRACY Cuff Links
135 TRUDIE Joe Henderson
136 VALERIE Steve Winwood
137 VALLERI Monkees
138 VANESSA Ted Heath
139 VICTORIA Kinks
140 WENDY Beach Boys

BOYS' NAMES WHICH BECAME SONG TITLES

Compared with the proliferation of girls' names used for song titles, those of the male gender provide much sparser pickings. Abiding by the same rules as the female list (i.e. no additional words in the title), the following list of 25 almost represents the sum total of what we could discover:

1 ALFIE Cilla Black ★
2 ANGELO Brotherhood Of Man
3 BEN Michael Jackson ★
4 BILLY Kathy Linden
5 BOBBY Neil Scott
6 CAREY Joni Mitchell
7 DANIEL Elton John
8 DANNY Elvis Presley
9 DENIS Blondie
10 FRANKIE Connie Francis
11 FREDDIE Charlene
12 JAMIE Eddie Holland
13 JESSE Carly Simon
14 MICHAEL Highwaymen
15 MICKEY Toni Basil
16 NORMAN Sue Thompson
17 ROCKY Austin Roberts
18 RUPERT Jackie Lee
19 SAM Olivia Newton-John
20 TEDDY Connie Francis
21 TERRY Twinkle
22 TIMOTHY Buoys
23 TOMMY Reparata & The Delrons
24 TOBY Chi-Lites
25 VINCENT Don McLean

THE MOST GOLD RECORDS AWARDED TO ONE ACT

Although gold records represent different achievements in different parts of the world, in the USA — where they originated — they mark the singular achievement of selling more than one million copies of a single.

Elvis Presley began recording for RCA early in 1956, and remained with the label until his death in 1977. Scarcely a year passed during that period when he did not release a single which passed the million sales mark, either domestically or on a global basis. Certain singles actually picked up multiple awards internationally — 'It's Now Or Never', for instance, also gained British and German gold discs for million-plus sales in those territories (this was long before the BPI award standardisations in Britain, under which a gold disc come to represent a half-million sale, with a platinum award indicating the million).

This list below itemises each Presley gold-awarded single, but lists them once only, regardless of how many additional awards individual releases may have picked up. Several of his hits sold in excess of two million units, and long before the introduction of the RIAA platinum award for this total in 1976, it was RCA's habit to award a second gold disc for the additional seven figures. This second award normally credited the title of the flipside of the single, which was usually a material factor in the achievement of the total sale, particularly in Presley's case. Singles on which both sides played a major part in this way are listed as double-siders, as are those where both sides contributed more or less equally to a single million sale.

1 HEARTBREAK HOTEL (1956)
2 I WANT YOU, I NEED YOU, I LOVE YOU (1956)
3 DON'T BE CRUEL/HOUND DOG (1956)
4 LOVE ME TENDER (1956)
5 LOVE ME (EP) (1956)
6 TOO MUCH (1957)
7 ALL SHOOK UP (1957)
8 (LET ME BE YOUR) TEDDY BEAR (1957)
9 JAILHOUSE ROCK (1957)
10 DON'T (1958)
11 WEAR MY RING AROUND YOUR NECK (1958)
12 HARD HEADED WOMAN (1958)
13 ONE NIGHT/I GOT STUNG (1958)
14 I NEED YOUR LOVE TONIGHT/A FOOL SUCH AS I (1959)
15 A BIG HUNK O' LOVE (1959)
16 STUCK ON YOU (1960)
17 IT'S NOW OR NEVER (1960)
18 ARE YOU LONESOME TONIGHT? (1960)
19 SURRENDER (1961)

BRITISH RECORDS WHICH REACHED NO. 1 IN THE US WITHOUT CHARTING IN THE UK

EIGHT DAYS A WEEK Beatles (1965)
MRS. BROWN YOU'VE GOT A LOVELY
 DAUGHTER Herman's Hermits (1965)
I'M HENRY VIII, I AM Herman's Hermits (1965)
TO SIR WITH LOVE Lulu (1967)
THE LONG AND WINDING ROAD Beatles (1970)
HOW CAN YOU MEND A BROKEN HEART
 Bee Gees (1971)
UNCLE ALBERT/ADMIRAL HALSEY
 Paul & Linda McCartney (1971)
HAVE YOU NEVER BEEN MELLOW
 Olivia Newton-John (1975) ★
(LOVE IS) THICKER THAN WATER Andy Gibb (1978)

The Beatles', Herman's Hermits' and Paul McCartney's tracks were not released as singles in Britain, and therefore stood no chance of charting! Lulu's 'To Sir With Love' was the British B-side of her single 'Let's Pretend', promoted later as an American A-side when the film of the same name was released in the US.

There is no explanation for the UK failure of the other three titles, except that they simply did not register with British record buyers. It presumably could have had nothing to do with the fact that the acts in question all grew up in Australia (could it?).

SINGLES WHICH HAVE ENTERED THE BRITISH CHARTS AT NUMBER ONE

1 JAILHOUSE ROCK Elvis Presley (24 Jan 1958)
2 I GOT STUNG/ONE NIGHT Elvis Presley (24 Jan 1959)
3 MY OLD MAN'S A DUSTMAN Lonnie Donegan (26 Mar 1960)
4 IT'S NOW OR NEVER Elvis Presley (5 Nov 1960)
5 SURRENDER Elvis Presley (27 May 1961)
6 THE YOUNG ONES Cliff Richard & The Shadows (11 Jan 1962)
7 I WANT TO HOLD YOUR HAND Beatles (7 Dec 1963)
8 CAN'T BUY ME LOVE Beatles (28 Mar 1964)
9 A HARD DAY'S NIGHT Beatles (18 Jul 1964)
10 I FEEL FINE Beatles (5 Dec 1964)
11 TICKET TO RIDE Beatles (17 Apr 1965)
12 HELP! Beatles (31 Jul 1965)
13 DAY TRIPPER/WE CAN WORK IT OUT Beatles (11 Dec 1965)

14 GET BACK Beatles with Billy Preston (23 Apr 1969)
15 CUM ON FEEL THE NOIZE Slade (3 Mar 1973)
16 SKWEEZE ME PLEEZE ME Slade (30 Jun 1973)
17 I LOVE YOU, LOVE ME LOVE Gary Glitter
   (17 Nov 1973)
18 MERRY XMAS EVERYBODY Slade (15 Dec 1973)
19 GOING UNDERGROUND/DREAMS OF
   CHILDREN Jam (22 Mar 1980)
20 DON'T STAND SO CLOSE TO ME
   Police (27 Sep 1980)
21 STAND AND DELIVER
   Adam & The Ants (9 May 1981)
22 TOWN CALL MALICE/PRECIOUS
   Jam (13 Feb 1982)
23 BEAT SURRENDER Jam (4 Dec 1982)
24 IS THERE SOMETHING I SHOULD KNOW?
   Duran Duran (26 Mar 1983)★

The first British chart to feature a No. 1 first-week entry (by 'Jailhouse Rock') is shown elsewhere in this book. The number of artists who have achieved the feat is inevitably small, with The Beatles (8 titles), Elvis Presley (4), Slade and The Jam (3 each) being the only ones to have repeated their triumph.

It should be noted by chart statisticians that a variety of charts were consulted to compile this listing. The pre-BMRB *Music Week/ Record Retailer* chart in the 1960s was compiled at a point in the week which barely caught first-week sales of new releases, so the first 13 titles on the list are those which entered at No 1 in the other UK charts compiled by the *NME, Melody Maker, Disc* and *Record Mirror*, which were regarded as equally important and valid in those days.

FEMALE ARTISTS TO HAVE RECORDED FOR LABELS RUN BY THEIR HUSBANDS

SANDIE SHAW for Palace (UK), run by Nik Powell
SHELLEY FABARES for Dunhill (USA), run by Lou Adler
NATASHA for Towerbell (UK), run by Bob England ★
RONNIE SPECTOR for Phil Spector Int. (USA),
    run by Phil Spector
CLAIRE HAMMILL for Beggars Banquet (UK),
    run by Nick Austin
LANI HALL for A&M (USA), run by Herb Alpert
YOKO ONO for Apple (UK), co-run by John Lennon
    with the other Beatles
JANET BLEYER (as a soloist and a member of the
    Chordettes) for Cadence (USA), run by Archie Bleyer
TERESA BREWER for Flying Dutchman (USA),
    run by Bob Thiele
MARY HOPKIN for Good Earth (UK),
    run by Tony Visconti ★

Hardly nepotism run wild here, as the ladies above are all recognised artists, quite apart from the fact that they do record, or have recorded, for hubby's company. If you had both a record label and a talented wife, you wouldn't miss the opportunity either.

THE CHART THEY GOT WRONG

In February 1976, the British Market Research Bureau (compiling the official UK industry chart at the time) had an aberration in its computer system which resulted in an incorrect compilation of the singles chart. The fault was noticed and rectified, but not until the incorrect version of the chart had been released to the BBC, who announced the placings over the air. Three hours later that chart was officially cancelled and the BBC re-announced the accurate version.

Below is the incorrect chart which gave Manuel & His Music Of The Mountains the all-time shortest residence at the No. 1 slot — just three hours. The top 20 positions are given, together with (on the far right) the finally corrected position for each of these entries:

1	(8)	RODRIGO'S GUITAR CONCERTO D'ARANJUEZ Manuel & His Music Of The Mountains	(4)
2	(23)	I LOVE TO LOVE Tina Charles	(3)
3	(3)	DECEMBER '63 (OH WHAT A NIGHT) Four Seasons	(1)
4	(1)	FOREVER AND EVER Slik	(2)
5	(21)	IT SHOULD HAVE BEEN ME Yvonne Fair	(14)
6	(7)	NO REGRETS Walker Brothers	(11)
7	(25)	LET'S CALL IT QUITS Slade	(18)
8	(41)	CONVOY C.W. McCall	(7)
9	(6)	WE DO IT R & J Stone	(9)
10	(29)	DAT Pluto Shervington	(10)
11	(17)	MOONLIGHT SERENADE Glenn Miller	(13)
12	(2)	MAMMA MIA Abba ★	(5)
13	(19)	SQUEEZE BOX Who	(15)
14	(10)	WALK AWAY FROM LOVE David Ruffin	(16)
15	(36)	RAIN Status Quo	(17)
16	(4)	LOVE MACHINE Miracles	(8)
17	(12)	BABY FACE Wing & A Prayer Fife & Drum Corps	(19)
18	(30)	I LOVE MUSIC O'Jays	(20)
19	(27)	SOMETHING'S BEEN MAKING ME BLUE Smokie	(21)
20	(44)	FUNKY WEEKEND Stylistics	(22)

The reinstatements in the corrected top 20 were 'Love To Love You Baby' by Donna Summer at No.6 (it had been No. 5 the previous week, anyway!), and 'Low Rider' by War at No. 12.

THE BEE GEES-DOMINATED AMERICAN TOP 10

On March 18, 1978, The Bee Gees in assorted capacities secured a stranglehold at the top of the American singles chart which almost matched The Beatles' occupation of the entire top five, 14 years earlier. This is the chart, from the combined rankings of Billboard and Cash Box magazines:

1 (4) NIGHT FEVER Bee Gees
2 (3) EMOTION Samantha Sang
3 (2) STAYIN' ALIVE Bee Gees
4 (1) (LOVE IS) THICKER THAN WATER Andy Gibb
5 (6) LAY DOWN SALLY Eric Clapton
6 (11) CAN'T SMILE WITHOUT YOU Barry Manilow
7 (5) SOMETIMES WHEN WE TOUCH Dan Hill
8 (9) I GO CRAZY Paul Davis
9 (10) WHAT'S YOUR NAME Lynryd Skynryd
10 (14) THUNDER ISLAND Jay Ferguson

In addition to the group's own two singles at Nos. 1 and 3, the single they replaced at the top and sent down to No. 4 was by their younger brother Andy, while Samantha Sang's 'Emotion' at No. 2 was written and produced by Barry Gibb, and the group are strongly featured on back-up vocals.

THE BEATLES-DOMINATED AMERICAN TOP 10

On March 28, 1964, at the height of the first wave of Beatlemania in the USA, the Beatles achieved the unprecedented (and unlikely ever to be equalled) feat of placing five of their singles in the top five positions on the American top 100. At the time, they had already monopolised the number one slot for nine straight weeks (seven with 'I Want To Hold Your Hand', two with 'She Loves You'), and during the following week 'Can't Buy Me Love' was due to start a five-week stint there. From February 22 for four weeks the group took the top two positions on the chart; on March 14 they had the top three plus No. 6; on March 21 they held No. 1 to 4. March 28, however, was the history-making week, and this was the top ten, from the combined rankings of Billboard and Cash Box magazines:

1 (3) TWIST AND SHOUT Beatles
2 (23) CAN'T BUY ME LOVE Beatles
3 (1) SHE LOVES YOU Beatles
4 (2) I WANT TO HOLD YOUR HAND Beatles
5 (4) PLEASE PLEASE ME Beatles
6 (7) HELLO DOLLY Louis Armstrong
7 (12) SUSPICION Terry Stafford
8 (8) MY HEART BELONGS TO ONLY YOU
        Bobby Vinton
9 (5) DAWN (GO AWAY) Four Seasons
10 (10) GLAD ALL OVER Dave Clark Five

The single at No. 6, Louis Armstrong's 'Hello Dolly', did eventually get to number one, making the veteran jazz trumpeter the first American artist to break the 15-week Beatle embargo at the chart top.

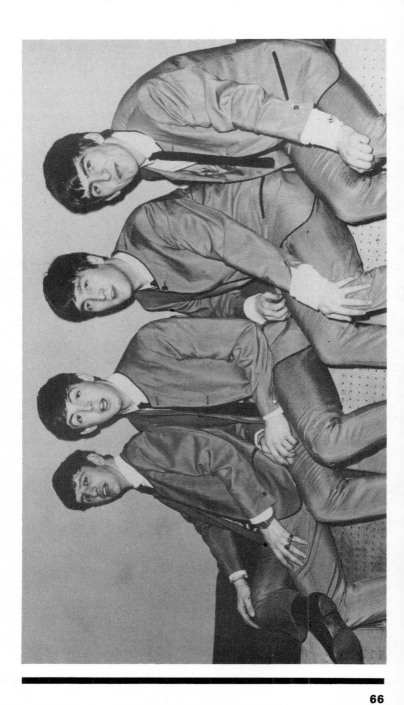

THE BRITISH TOP 20 OF WHICH THE BEATLES TOOK A QUARTER SHARE

There was a period in April 1976 when EMI re-promoted the entire Beatles singles catalogue; they managed six titles in the top 50 simultaneously, with a further dozen or so in the second half of the top 100, which was not published. Thirteen years earlier, however, the group had managed to place five titles simultaneously in the top 20, achieving the feat with a staggering mixture of two singles (at Nos. 1 and 2), two EPs and their second album – which was included in most singles charts of the time to emphasise the strength of its sales against the normally fairly insignificant LP sales of the day.

The week in question saw the chart debut of 'I Want To Hold Your Hand', at No. 1. The group had also had five entries in the top 20 during the previous week, however, with yet another EP, 'The Beatles No. 1' (selling on the strength of lead track 'I Saw Her Standing There'), at No. 19. In the chart listed below (w/e December 7, 1963), it dropped to No. 29, still giving The Beatles six titles in the top 30:

1 (-)   I WANT TO HOLD YOUR HAND Beatles
2 (1)   SHE LOVES YOU Beatles

3 (6)   YOU WERE MADE FOR ME Freddie and The Dreamers
4 (2)   DON'T TALK TO HIM Cliff Richard & The Shadows
5 (5)   SECRET LOVE Kathy Kirby
6 (3)   YOU'LL NEVER WALK ALONE Gerry & The Pacemakers
7 (4)   I'LL KEEP YOU SATISFIED
        Billy J. Kramer & The Dakotas
8 (9)   MARIA ELENA Los Indios Tabajaras
9 (15) GLAD ALL OVER Dave Clark Five
10 (13) I ONLY WANT TO BE WITH YOU Dusty Springfield

11 (17) WITH THE BEATLES (LP) Beatles

12 (12) IT'S ALMOST TOMORROW Mark Wynter
13 (8) BE MY BABY Ronettes
14 (7) SUGAR AND SPICE Searchers

15 (16) TWIST AND SHOUT (EP) Beatles
16 (20) THE BEATLES' HITS (EP) Beatles

17 (33) DOMINIQUE Singing Nun
18 (10) I (WHO HAVE NOTHING) Shirley Bassey
19 (11) BLUE BAYOU Roy Orbison
20 (22) MONEY Bern Elliott & The Fenmen

THE MOST SIMULTANEOUS TOP 30 HITS BY ONE ARTIST IN THE UK CHART

The maximum number of simultaneous entries in the top 30 of the UK chart ever achieved by one act totalled eight (almost a third of the chart!). The record was set in the week ending November 1, 1957, by Elvis Presley. Two weeks earlier, Elvis had had five simultaneous top 20 entries, a feat which Bill Haley had managed a year earlier, and which The Beatles would later equal; but nobody else is ever likely to come close to this top 30 record. Somewhat ironically, Elvis also holds the record for simultaneous top 50 entries — just after his death in August 1977, ten of his singles reoccupied the charts, though mostly in positions below the top 30.

This is the top 30 chart of November 1, 1957:

1 (2) THAT'LL BE THE DAY Crickets
2 (1) DIANA Paul Anka
3 (3) (LET'S HAVE A) PARTY Elvis Presley
4 (4) TAMMY Debbie Reynolds
5 (6) REMEMBER YOU'RE MINE Pat Boone
6 (5) LOVE LETTERS IN THE SAND Pat Boone
7 (14) MAN ON FIRE/WANDERIN' EYES Frankie Vaughan
8 (13) WHOLE LOTTA SHAKIN' GOIN' ON Jerry Lee Lewis
9 (19) BE MY GIRL Jim Dale
10 (7) WANDERIN' EYES Charlie Gracie
11 (9) TEDDY BEAR Elvis Presley
12 (8) ISLAND IN THE SUN Harry Belafonte
13 (10) WATER, WATER/HANDFUL OF SONGS Tommy Steele
14 (15) MY DIXIE DARLING Lonnie Donegan
15 (11) WITH ALL MY HEART Petula Clark
16 (12) LAST TRAIN TO SAN FERNANDO Johnny Duncan
17 (16) ALL SHOOK UP Elvis Presley
18 (17) CALL ROSIE ON THE PHONE Guy Mitchell
19 (18) GOT A LOT O' LIVIN' TO DO Elvis Presley
20 (22) STARDUST Billy Ward & The Dominoes
21 (-) TRYING TO GET TO YOU Elvis Presley
22 (-) GOTTA HAVE SOMETHING IN THE BANK, FRANK
         Frankie Vaughan & The Kaye Sisters
23 (23) SHORT FAT FANNIE Larry Williams
24 (28) LOVING YOU Elvis Presley
25 (21) WEDDING RING Russ Hamilton
26 (20) PARALYSED Elvis Presley
27 (27) STARDUST Nat "King" Cole
28 (-) BLUE BLUE HEARTACHES Johnny Duncan
29 (-) HONEYCOMB Jimmie Rodgers
30 (-) LAWDY MISS CLAWDY Elvis Presley

30 MILLION-SELLING FILM TITLE SONGS (where the version as used in the movie became a hit single)

1 A HARD DAY'S NIGHT Beatles
2 A STAR IS BORN (EVERGREEN) Barbra Streisand
3 APRIL LOVE Pat Boone
4 ARTHUR'S THEME (BEST THAT YOU CAN DO) Christopher Cross
5 CAR WASH Rose Royce
6 CATCH US IF YOU CAN Dave Clark Five
7 CHARIOTS OF FIRE Vangelis
8 ENDLESS LOVE Diana Ross & Lionel Richie
9 EVERY WHICH WAY BUT LOOSE Eddie Rabbitt
10 FAME Irene Cara
11 FERRY CROSS THE MERSEY Gerry & The Pacemakers
12 FLASHDANCE (WHAT A FEELING) Irene Cara
13 FOR YOUR EYES ONLY Sheena Easton
14 GEORGY GIRL Seekers
15 GOLDFINGER Shirley Bassey ★
16 GREASE Frankie Valli
17 HELP! Beatles
18 JAILHOUSE ROCK Elvis Presley
19 LET IT BE Beatles
20 LOVE ME TENDER Elvis Presley
21 NINE TO FIVE Dolly Parton
22 ROCK AROUND THE CLOCK Bill Haley & The Comets
23 SUPERFLY Curtis Mayfield
24 THE HAPPENING Supremes
25 THE WAY WE WERE Barbra Streisand
26 THE YOUNG ONES Cliff Richard
27 THEME FROM SHAFT Isaac Hayes
28 TO SIR WITH LOVE Lulu
29 WHAT'S NEW PUSSYCAT? Tom Jones
30 XANADU Olivia Newton-John & Electric Light Orchestra

The above is not an exhaustive list, but it does cover most of the original soundtrack themes which were million-plus sellers. Additionally, many acts have had enormous hits with their own non-soundtrack versions of movie titles, familiar examples being Hugo Montenegro with *The Good, The Bad & The Ugly*, Percy Faith with *Theme From A Summer Place*, Dionne Warwick with *Alfie*, and Booker T & The MGs with *Hang 'em High*.

NO IMAGINATION

Fifty acts whose first album title was nothing more nor less than their own name:

1 AMERICA (1972)
2 THE ANIMALS (1964)
3 BAD COMPANY (1974)
4 BIG BROTHER & THE HOLDING COMPANY (1967)
5 BLACK SABBATH (1970)
6 BOSTON (1977)
7 BREAD (1969)
8 CREEDENCE CLEARWATER REVIVAL (1968)
9 CROSBY, STILLS & NASH (1969)
10 THE DOORS (1967)
11 BOB DYLAN (1962)
12 EMERSON, LAKE & PALMER (1970)
13 GRATEFUL DEAD (1967)
14 PETER GABRIEL (1977) — Gabriel's second and third albums were also titled 'Peter Gabriel'
15 HOT TUNA (1970)
16 KINKS (1964)
17 LED ZEPPELIN (1969)
18 BRENDA LEE (1960)
19 LOVE (1966)
20 THE MONKEES (1966)
21 THE MOVE (1966)
22 NAZARETH (1971)
23 NEW RIDERS OF THE PURPLE SAGE (1971)
24 THE ONLY ONES (1978)
25 ORCHESTRAL MANOEUVRES IN THE DARK (1980)
26 OSIBISA (1971)
27 PENTANGLE (1968)

This is by no means an exhaustive list, merely the best-known perpetrators of the cop-out title. By way of variation, several other acts managed to hold on until their second album before they ran out of imagination, title-wise; for example: Traffic, Elton John, The Ventures, The Band, The Mamas & The Papas, and Chicago (though that last one is a whole different story, as fully documented in volume one of this series). Perhaps special awards for not-taking-the-easy-way-out should be given, however, to the likes of The Beatles, who waited until their white double album in 1968 before using that title, and to Cliff Richard, who had recorded 12 albums prior to going for the easy one in 1965.

HOW BEATLE FANS RATED THEIR SONGS

In 1965 and 1966, the officially-approved *Beatles Book* conducted polls among its readers to determine Beatle fans' preferences among the songs on their then-current albums. The November 1965 edition published the results of the *Help!* album poll, and the November 1966 issue had the *Revolver* results. American readers should bear in mind that these polls were based upon the contents of the British versions of these albums, which had more tracks than their American counterparts.

THE HELP LP SONG POLL

1 YESTERDAY
2 YOU'VE GOT TO HIDE YOUR LOVE AWAY
3 YOU'RE GOING TO LOSE THAT GIRL
4 ANOTHER GIRL
5 I NEED YOU
6 THE NIGHT BEFORE
7 I'VE JUST SEEN A FACE
8 YOU LIKE ME TOO MUCH
9 HELP
10 IT'S ONLY LOVE
11 ACT NATURALLY
12 TELL ME WHAT YOU SEE
13 DIZZY MISS LIZZY
14 TICKET TO RIDE

THE REVOLVER LP POLL

1 HERE, THERE AND EVERYWHERE
2 ELEANOR RIGBY
3 FOR NO ONE
4 I'M ONLY SLEEPING
5 GOT TO GET YOU INTO MY LIFE
6 GOOD DAY SUNSHINE
7 AND YOUR BIRD CAN SING
8 YELLOW SUBMARINE
9 TOMORROW NEVER KNOWS
10 LOVE YOU TO
11 TAXMAN
12 I WANT TO TELL YOU
13 DR ROBERT
14 SHE SAID, SHE SAID

Alongside the *Help* poll, the magazine also printed the result of a poll to find readers' all-time favourite Beatle songs to date (up to summer 1965), and the following are the 20 titles which led the field at that time:

1 HELP
2 ALL MY LOVING
3 SHE LOVES YOU
4 I'M DOWN
5 THIS BOY
6 A HARD DAY'S NIGHT
7 YESTERDAY
8 TWIST AND SHOUT
9 IF I FELL
10 TICKET TO RIDE
11 YES IT IS
12 EIGHT DAYS A WEEK
13 YOU'VE GOT TO HIDE YOUR LOVE AWAY
14 I WANT TO HOLD YOUR HAND
15 AND I LOVE HER
16 CAN'T BUY ME LOVE
17 I FEEL FINE
18 SHE'S A WOMAN
19 P.S. I LOVE YOU
20 I'M A LOSER

The voting was probably coloured by the fact that 'Help'/'I'm Down' was The Beatles' current single at the time. Odd, however, that both 'Help' and 'Ticket To Ride' should have rated so highly in this overall listing when they scored comparatively poorly in the *Help* album poll taken at the same time. Maybe different fans voted?

MORE BEATLE FANS' SONG RATINGS

In 1976, some eleven years after the *Beatles Book* all-time favourite song poll, and several years after The Beatles had actually broken up (thereby giving some historical perspective to the voting), the American magazine *Survey* asked Beatle fans to nominate their all-time favourites. Below are the top 15 choices:

1 SGT. PEPPER'S LONELY HEARTS CLUB BAND/
   A DAY IN THE LIFE (i.e., the full segued sequence at the end of the Sgt. Pepper album)
2 HEY JUDE
3 YESTERDAY
4 LET IT BE
5 HELP!
6 ALL MY LOVING
7 THE LONG AND WINDING ROAD
8 SHE LOVES YOU
9 IF I FELL
10 AND I LOVE HER
11 ELEANOR RIGBY
12 BACK IN THE USSR
13 LADY MADONNA
14 A HARD DAY'S NIGHT
15 I AM THE WALRUS

The pollsters here, of course, were largely American, whereas the previous poll had used mostly British voters. Nevertheless, 'Yesterday', 'All My Loving', 'She Loves You', 'Help!' and 'If I Fell' in particular, can be seen to have maintained their popularity despite all that came later.

More or less midway between the 60s *Beatles Book* poll and the 1976 *Survey* one, Howard Smith — a DJ on radio station WPLJ and writer for the *Village Voice* magazine — asked for votes in a poll to find the least popular Beatle song. These were the top five, not showing anything very surprising:

1 REVOLUTION No. 9
2 MR MOONLIGHT
3 YOU KNOW MY NAME (LOOK UP THE NUMBER)
4 HELTER SKELTER
5 DO YOU WANT TO KNOW A SECRET

THE MOST MOVIE-FEATURED BEATLE

The following is a list of the movie appearances of Ringo Starr, who took to acting in films as easily as he had earlier fallen into musical superstardom. The first four titles below feature Ringo with the other Beatles; the remainder are all solo appearances:

A HARD DAY'S NIGHT
HELP!
YELLOW SUBMARINE
   (brief cameo at end of cartoon only)
LET IT BE
CANDY
THE MAGIC CHRISTIAN
200 MOTELS
BLINDMAN
BORN TO BOOGIE (the T.Rex documentary
   he directed, and appeared in briefly)
THAT'LL BE THE DAY
SON OF DRACULA
LISZTOMANIA
CAVEMAN

Ringo also appeared, of course, together with the other Beatles in *Magical Mystery Tour*, a TV film special which was never given a cinematic release.

THE TEN ARRANGERS ON RINGO STARR'S 'SENTIMENTAL JOURNEY' ALBUM

When Ringo decided in 1969 to make a solo album of standards, dedicated to his mother, he spread his suggestions for the tracks out among ten friends, inviting them to test out their talents on big-band-type arrangements to suit the material.

The album was originally to have been called 'Ringo Starrdust', but it appeared early in 1970 as *Sentimental Journey,* containing 12 "oldies" like 'Whispering Grass', 'Love Is A Many-Splendoured Thing', 'Stardust', and 'Night And Day'. It probably holds the record for the album with the most different all-star arrangers, because all ten friends came back to do a track or so apiece. They were:

RICHARD PERRY
QUINCY JONES
GEORGE MARTIN
RON GOODWIN
MAURICE GIBB
JOHN DANKWORTH
KLAUS VOORMAN
ELMER BERNSTEIN
LES REED
PAUL McCARTNEY

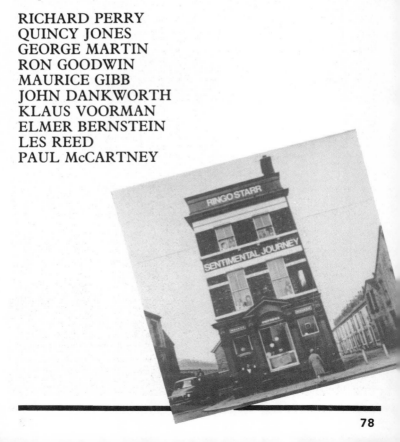

TEN PLACES MARI WILSON WOULD MOST LIKE TO LIVE

1 AMSTERDAM
2 NEASDEN, LONDON
3 NEW YORK
4 SPAIN
5 SCOTLAND
6 GREEK ISLANDS
7 SRI LANKA
8 THE LAKE DISTRICT
9 A DESERTED ISLAND
10 BARBADOS

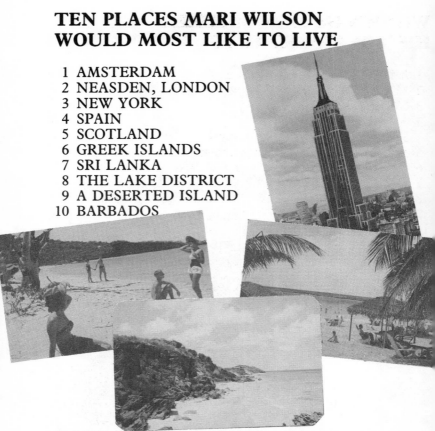

DAVID GRANT'S TEN FAVOURITE MAKES OF CAR

1 MASERATI COUNTACH
2 JAGUAR XJS HE
3 PORSCHE 933
4 FERRARI MONDIAL
5 MERCEDES 500 SEL
6 BMW 635 CS1
7 ASTON MARTIN
8 JAGUAR 5.3 XJ HE
9 MORRIS MINOR
10 1961 FORD PREFECT

WHAM'S GEORGE MICHAEL –
HIS TOP TEN SINGLES

1 MIRACLES – Love Machine
2 SUPREMES – Baby Love ★
3 SWEET – Hell Raiser
4 MICHAEL JACKSON –
 Don't Stop 'til You Get Enough
5 DAVID BOWIE – Young Americans
6 DOLLAR – Give Me Back My Heart
7 FUNKADELIC – One Nation Under A Groove
8 DOOBIE BROTHERS – What A Fool Believes
9 ABC – The Look Of Love
10 GAP BAND – Burn Rubber On Me

WHAM'S ANDY RIDGELEY –
HIS FAVOURITE THINGS

1 GEORGE AND SHIRLIE
2 MY MUM AND DAD
3 MY CAR
4 ME
5 WHAM!
6 GIRLS!
7 FOOD ★
8 FOSTERS
9 FILMS
10 SLEEP

SAXON'S GRAHAM OLIVER'S FAVOURITE SINGLES

1 JIMI HENDRIX − All Along The Watchtower ★
2 MOTT THE HOOPLE − All The Young Dudes
3 ALICE COOPER − School's Out
4 SAXON − 747 (Strangers In The Night)
5 JIMI HENDRIX − Purple Haze
6 OZZY OSBOURNE − Mr. Crowley
7 BEATLES − Hey Jude
8 ROLLING STONES − It's All Over Now
9 BOB DYLAN − Like A Rolling Stone
10 JOE COCKER − With A Little Help From My Friends

ALEXIS KORNER'S TEN FAVOURITE PIECES OF BLACK MUSIC

1 MUDDY WATERS − Louisiana Blues
2 ROBERT JOHNSON − Come On In My Kitchen
3 GEORGE COLEMAN − Eloise
4 MELODIANS − Rivers Of Babylon
5 BOB MARLEY − Bend Down Low
6 CANNONBALL ADDERLEY − Oh! Babe
7 JAMES BROWN − Kansas City
8 SLY STONE − Thank You, Africa
9 DUKE ELLINGTON − Time's A-Wasting
10 JIMMY REED − Big Boss Man

NICK HEYWARD'S FAVOURITE MAKES OF UNDERPANTS

1 MARKS AND SPENCER'S
2 BRITISH HOMESTORES
3 JONES
4 WOOLWORTHS
5 TOP SHOP
6 CHICKEN MADRAS
7 JANET REGER SPECIALS
8 BECKENHAM HIGH STREET SCHOOL SHOP
9 DAMART
10 VAUXHALL

KIM WILDE'S TEN FAVOURITE THINGS

1 JAPANESE FOOD
2 'ANYONE WHO HAD A HEART'
  BY CILLA BLACK
3 BILKO★
4 LONDON
5 MY FRIENDS
6 MY SWEET MEMORIES
7 DISCOVERING
8 YOGA AND WORKING
  OUT
9 MIRRORS AND THINGS
  THAT SHINE
10 SNOW STORMS

BANANARAMA'S KEREN WOODWARD'S FAVOURITE DRINKS

1 CORONA CHERRYADE
2 CORONA LIMEADE
3 TEA★
4 INSTANT COFFEE
5 VODKA & TONIC
6 VODKA & ORANGE
7 LAGER & BLACK
8 COLD MILK
9 LEMON BARLEY WATER
10 WATER

BANANARAMA'S SIOBHAN FAHEY'S FAVOURITE DOGS

1 BOXER
2 KING CHARLES SPANIEL
3 STAFFORDSHIRE BULL TERRIER
4 GREAT DANE
5 GOLDEN RETRIEVER
6 IRISH WOLFHOUND
7 SPANIEL
8 ST. BERNARD
9 SHITZU
10 'SCARTEEN' – A MIXTURE OF THE ABOVE

MARTIN RUSHENT'S FAVOURITE PRODUCTIONS

1 RIGHTEOUS BROTHERS — ★
   You've Lost That
   Lovin' Feelin'
2 IKE & TINA TURNER — River Deep Mountain High
3 JOHN LENNON — Imagine
4 CLIFF RICHARD — High Class Baby
5 BEATLES — Strawberry Fields Forever
6 MIRACLES — Tracks Of My Tears
7 OTIS REDDING — (Sittin' On The) Dock Of The Bay
8 SEX PISTOLS — Anarchy In The U.K.
9 ROLLING STONES — The Last Time
10 DURAN DURAN — Girls On Film

TWENTY ACTS WHO REACHED NUMBER ONE WITH THEIR FIRST HIT

Firstly, American acts who did it in the US charts:

LESLEY GORE with 'It's My Party' (1963)
TOMMY JAMES & THE SHONDELLS with 'Hanky Panky' (1966)
GARY LEWIS & THE PLAYBOYS with 'This Diamond Ring' (1965)
MONKEES with 'Last Train to Clarksville' (1966)★
JEANNIE C. RILEY with 'Harper Valley PTA' (1968)
DEL SHANNON with 'Runaway' (1961)
SIMON & GARFUNKEL with 'The Sound Of Silence' (1965)
PERCY SLEDGE with 'When A Man Loves A Woman' (1966)
TEDDY BEARS with 'To Know Him Is To Love Him' (1958)
STEVIE WONDER with 'Fingertips (Part 2)' (1963)

KATE BUSH with 'Wuthering Heights' (1978)★
FOUNDATIONS with 'Baby Now That I've Found You' (1967)
GERRY & THE PACEMAKERS with 'How Do You Do It' (1963)
HONEYCOMBS with 'Have I The Right' (1964)
MARY HOPKIN with 'Those Were The Days' (1968)
MUNGO JERRY with 'In The Summertime' (1970)
PETER & GORDON with 'A World Without Love' (1964)
PROCOL HARUM with 'A Whiter Shade Of Pale' (1967)
MIKE SARNE with 'Come Outside' (1962)
RICKY VALANCE with 'Tell Laura I Love Her' (1960)

A lot of these acts went on to very substantial hit-making careers. Gerry & The Pacemakers went on to set a record by topping the charts with their second and third hits too. The Monkees also had another chart-topper with their second US entry, 'I'm A Believer'. One-hit wonder of the batch was Ricky Valance who, despite topping the UK chart on his first attempt, never managed to place another single in the top 50.

THE FEW:

The acts who have topped the American and British singles and album charts simultaneously, with the *same* single and album.

BEATLES	A Hard Day's Night	
	A Hard Day's Night (LP)	August 1964
BEATLES	We Can Work It Out	
	Rubber Soul (LP)	January 1966
MONKEES	I'm A Believer	
	More Of The Monkees (LP)	February 1967
SIMON & GARFUNKEL		
	Bridge Over Troubled Water	
	Bridge Over Troubled Water (LP)	April 1970
ROD STEWART ★	Maggie May	
	Every Picture Tells A Story (LP)	October 1971
BEE GEES	Night Fever	
	Saturday Night Fever (LP)	May 1978
MEN AT WORK	Down Under	
	Business As Usual (LP)	January 1983
MICHAEL JACKSON	Billie Jean	
	Thriller (LP)	March 1983

On two further occasions in 1964 and 1965, The Beatles topped all four charts, but the two American albums in these cases – *Meet The Beatles* and *Beatles '65* – differed from the UK counterparts *With The Beatles* and *Beatles For Sale*, and so do not strictly count.

THE FIRST BRITISH MUSIC INDUSTRY CHART

Throughout the 1950s and most of the 60s, the leading weekly pop papers and the trade journal *Record Retailer* all compiled their own best-selling singles charts. Since they were based on different samplings of shops, each told a slightly different story; nevertheless, they all reflected the same broad picture, and the BBC took advantage of this by compiling its own broadcast chart from a statistical analysis of four published ones.

However, during 1968, the official British record industry body, the BPI, plus the BBC and *Record Retailer,* went into partnership to promote an official all-industry chart, and they hired a market research company, BMRB, to put it together using a sophisticated diary and computer system. The first chart was published in the week ending February 15, 1969, and BMRB continued to produce the industry chart by similar means up until the end of 1982, when the job was taken over by another research company, Gallup, using wholly computerised methods.

Below is the first BMRB singles top 50. The "last week" positions in brackets are those from the final chart compiled the previous week by *Record Retailer.*

1 (19) (IF PARADISE IS) HALF AS NICE Amen Corner
2 (2) ALBATROSS Fleetwood Mac
3 (1) BLACKBERRY WAY Move ★
4 (3) FOR ONCE IN MY LIFE Stevie Wonder
5 (4) DANCING IN THE STREET Martha & The Vandellas

35 (47) SHE'S NOT THERE Neil MacArthur
35 (37) A MINUTE OF YOUR TIME Tom Jones
37 (40) GENTLE ON MY MIND Dean Martin
38 (-) ALL THE LOVE IN THE WORLD Consortium
39 (41) SABRE DANCE Love Sculpture
39 (-) I HEARD IT THROUGH THE GRAPEVINE Marvin Gaye
41 (-) SURROUND YOURSELF WITH SORROW Cilla Black ★
42 (35) RING OF FIRE Eric Burdon & The Animals
43 (23) LOVE CHILD Diana Ross & The Supremes
44 (33) LOVE STORY Jethro Tull
45 (27) AIN'T GOT NO-I GOT LIFE Nina Simone
45 (44) ON MOTHER KELLY'S DOORSTEP Danny LaRue
45 (49) AQUARIUS Paul Jones
45 (-) MAY I HAVE THE NEXT DREAM WITH YOU
        Malcolm Roberts
45 (-) RIVER DEEP, MOUNTAIN HIGH Ike And Tina Turner
50 (-) DOES ANYONE KNOW MY NAME Vince Hill

One immediate problem which was apparent in this first chart was that the system tended to throw up tied positions — note two No. 16's, two 19's, two 31's, two 35's, two 39's and five records tied at position 45. This obviously was not very satisfactory, though the system soon sorted it out.

If some of the titles on the chart seem to throw it out of historical perspective, it should be pointed out that the fad of the day was the reissue and repromotion of (mainly American) hits from earlier in the 60s. This accounts for the apparently anachronistic entries by Martha & The Vandellas, Edwin Starr, The Righteous Brothers, The Isley Brothers and Ike & Tina Turner.

Finally, because of the change-over between two different methods of data analysis, several records which had been on the way down the chart took a temporary step back upwards. This applies to the apparently fast-rising entries by The Scaffold, Hugo Montenegro, The Foundations, and The Kasenetz-Katz Singing Orchestral Circus.

BRITAIN'S FIRST R&B CHART

In mid-1965, in order to reflect the growing interest in (and sales of) rhythm & blues material in Britain, *Record Mirror* began to put together a chart specifically devoted to R&B singles, compiled from shops around the country which specialised in the genre or had an especially large customer interest in it. This chart is the ancestor of all the soul and disco charts which have appeared in specialist black music magazines and in the record industry trade press during the subsequent 18 years.

Since the compilers of this book are also involved in the compilation of today's Disco/Dance industry chart (as published in *Music Week*), it seems fitting to pay homage to its roots. Here is that first R&B singles chart as published in *Record Mirror* on July 3, 1965:

1 I CAN'T HELP MYSELF Four Tops
   (Tamla Motown TMG 515)
2 SHE'S ABOUT A MOVER Sir Douglas Quintet ★
   (London HLU 9964)
3 A LITTLE PIECE OF LEATHER
   Donnie Elbert (Sue WI 377)
4 MAGGIE'S FARM Solomon Burke (Atlantic AT 4630)
5 WOOLY BULLY
   Sam The Sham & The Pharoahs (MGM 1269)
6 MR PITIFUL Otis Redding (Atlantic AT 4024)
7 INCENSE Anglos (Fontana TF 589)
8 AND I LOVE HIM Esther Phillips (Atlantic AT 4028)
9 PEEPIN' Solomon Burke (Atlantic AT 4022)
10 NOTHING CAN STOP ME
   Gene Chandler (Stateside SS 425)
11 SHOTGUN Jr Walker & The All-Stars
   (Tamla Motown TMG 509)
12 DUST MY BLUES Elmore James (Sue WI 335)
13 DOWN HOME GIRL
   Alvin Robinson (Red Bird 10-010)

At the time, it was felt very important to include the catalogue number of each record on this chart, to help readers who were trying to get their local shops to order more specialist material for them. It was at the time quite a revolutionary move by a pop paper — and to keep in with the spirit of the thing, we've done the same.

BRITAIN'S LAST EP CHART

For many years, records sold in three formats in Britain — singles, albums, and four-track EPs. Although both albums and EPs sometimes reached the singles chart if their sales were sufficiently strong, there were also separate charts for each of these formats; the trade paper *Record Retailer* began a weekly top 20 listing for each in 1960. However, by 1967 — sometime after The Beatles in particular had sold vast quantities of EPs — production of the four-track format had almost dried up, probably due to the adverse effect on its sales from budget albums introduced to huge success by Music For Pleasure and Marble Arch. These offered ten or twelve tracks for little more than the cost of an EP, and virtually priced the four-tracker out of its market. The top 20 EP chart shrank to a top 10 as there were fewer discs to survey; and as the numbers of releases continued to shrink, it was finally decided to cease compilation altogether and increase the length of the album chart, which was reflecting a continually growing market.

The last top 10 EP chart appeared in *Record Retailer* and *Record Mirror* on December 16, 1967, and ran as follows:

1	(1)	BEACH BOYS' HITS Beach Boys
2	(2)	FOUR TOP HITS Four Tops
3	(4)	FOUR TOPS Four Tops
4	(3)	THE BEST OF BENNETT Tony Bennett
5	(6)	MORNINGTOWN RIDE Seekers
6	(9)	HITS FROM THE SEEKERS Seekers
7	(7)	PRIVILEGE (SOUNDTRACK) Paul Jones
8	(5)	EASY COME, EASY GO (SOUNDTRACK) Elvis Presley
9	(8)	GEORGIE FAME Georgie Fame
10	(10)	MIRIELLE MATHIEU Mirielle Mathieu

THE FIRST BRITISH DISCO CHART

1 THREE TIMES A LADY Commodores (Motown)★

2 GALAXY OF LOVE Crown Heights Affair (Mercury)
3 BRITISH HUSTLE Hi-Tension (Island)
4 LET THE MUSIC PLAY Charles Earland (Mercury)
5 YOU MAKE ME FEEL (MIGHTY REAL)
     Sylvester (Fantasy)

6 LET'S START THE DANCE Bohannon (Mercury)
7 SUPERNATURE Cerrone (Atlantic)
8 I THOUGHT IT WAS YOU Herbie Hancock (CBS)
9 HOT SHOT Karen Young (Atlantic)
10 STUFF LIKE THAT Quincy Jones (A&M)
11 SHAME Evelyn "Champagne" King (RCA)
12 BOOGIE OOGIE OOGIE A Taste Of Honey (Capitol)
13 STANDING ON THE VERGE
   Platinum Hook (Motown)
14 THINK IT OVER Cissy Houston (Private Stock)
15 SOUL TO SOUL/MUSIC FEVER
   Michael Zager (Private Stock)
16 YOU AND I Rick James (Motown)
17 GOT A FEELING Patrick Juvet (Casablanca)
18 AN EVERLASTING LOVE Andy Gibb (RSO)
19 DO OR DIE Grace Jones (Island)
20 NIGHT FEVER Carol Douglas (Gull)
21 MAGIC MIND Earth, Wind & Fire (CBS)
22 WHAT YOU WAITIN' FOR Stargard (MCA)
23 YOUNGBLOOD War (United Artists)
24 GET OFF Foxy (TK)
25 DON'T STOP NOW Gene Farrow (Magnet)
26 DISCO INFERNO Trammps (Atlantic)
27 COPACABANA Barry Manilow (Arista)
28 DON'T WANNA SAY GOODNIGHT
   Kandidate (RAK)
29 COME BACK AND FINISH WHAT YOU STARTED
   Gladys Knight & The Pips (Buddah)
30 FROM EAST TO WEST Voyage (GTO)

The first British disco chart was introduced, like the first independent chart, by the trade paper *Record Business*. The chart was first published as a top 50 in the issue dated August 28th, 1978, and continued to be an important part of *Record Business*, until the paper ceased publication in February 1983. It has subsequently been published every week in *Music Week*, in addition to a top 30 Disco Album chart. Several radio stations have broadcast the chart, notably Capital Radio and Radio Luxembourg.

THE FIRST INDIE CHART

1 WHERE'S CAPTAIN KIRK?
  Spizzenergi (Rough Trade)★

 2 DAYTRIP TO BANGOR Fiddler's Dram (Dingle's)
 3 MIND YOUR OWN BUSINESS
   Delta Five (Rough Trade)
 4 WHITE MICE Mo-Dettes (Mode)
 5 CALIFORNIA UBER ALLES Dead Kennedys (Fast)
 6 TRANSMISSION Joy Division (Factory)
 7 EARCOM THREE (EP) Various (Fast)
 8 WE ARE ALL PROSTITUTES
   Pop Group (Rough Trade)
 9 KAMIKAZE Boys (Safari)
10 SILENT COMMAND Cabaret Voltaire (Rough Trade)
11 TAAGA (EP) Dangerous Girls (Happy Face)
12 BILL GRUNDY (EP) TV Personalities (Rough Trade)
13 HE'S FRANK (SLIGHT RETURN)
   Monochrome Set (Rough Trade)

14 SHEEP FARMING IN BARNET (AP) Toyah (Safari)★
15 YOU'VE NEVER HEARD ANYTHING LIKE IT
    Freshmen (Release)
16 I'M IN LOVE WITH MARGARET THATCHER
    Not Sensibles (Redball)
17 FOUR A-SIDES Scritti Politti (Rough Trade)
18 YOU CAN BE YOU Honey Bane (Crass)
19 SID DID IT Nazis Against Fascism (Truth)
20 PEEL SESSIONS Scritti Politti (Rough Trade)
21 REALITY ASYLUM Crass (Crass)
22 OPENING UP Circles (Graduate)
23 SOLDIER SOLDIER Spizzenergi (Rough Trade)
24 POPCORN BABY Essential Logic (Rough Trade)
25 CONFESSIONS Flowers (Pop Aural)
26 KISS THE MIRROR Wall (Small Wonder)
27 UK '79 Crisis (Ardkor)
28 FIRST AND LAST Art Attax (Fresh)
29 ADDICTS 4-TRACK (EP) Addicts (Dining Out)
30 GABRIELLE Nips (Soho)

Charts of records on independently-distributed labels are now an accepted part of the fabric of the British record industry. Since their inception in February 1980 in the trade paper *Record Business*, many important records and acts have crossed over from these listings to national and international success — including a couple of those shown in the chart above, which was the first to be compiled (by the present authors, as it happens...)

CHART-TOPPING REMAKES OF FORMER HIT SONGS

New versions of old hit songs frequently make the charts. Much less common are remakes that top the chart when an earlier hit version of the song (often, but not always, the original recording) failed to do so. The following is a list of records which achieved this feat in the UK charts. The act which had the original UK chart version is shown in brackets:

AMAZING GRACE
　　Royal Scots Dragoon Guards Band (Judy Collins)
BLUE MOON Marcels (Elvis Presley)
CRYING Don McLean (Roy Orbison) ★
CRYING IN THE CHAPEL Elvis Presley (Lee Lawrence)
EVERYTHING I OWN Ken Boothe (Bread) ✦
GREEN DOOR Shakin' Stevens (Frankie Vaughan)
HOW CAN I BE SURE David Cassidy (Dusty Springfield)

IT'S MY PARTY
   Dave Stewart & Barbara Gaskin (Lesley Gore) ★
OH BOY Mud (Crickets)
PUPPY LOVE Donny Osmond (Paul Anka)
THE FIRST CUT IS THE DEEPEST
   Rod Stewart (P.P. Arnold)
THE LION SLEEPS TONIGHT Tight Fit (Tokens)
THE TWELFTH OF NEVER
   Donny Osmond (Cliff Richard)
THE WAYWARD WIND Frank Ifield (Gogi Grant)
THE WONDER OF YOU Elvis Presley (Ray Peterson)
WORKING MY WAY BACK TO YOU
   Detroit Spinners (Four Seasons)

And now three songs with a unique achievement — namely, reaching number one in their first hit version, and then making the top again as a revival many years later:

MARY'S BOY CHILD Harry Belafonte (1957) and
   Boney M (1978)
THIS OLE HOUSE Rosemary Clooney (1954) and
   Shakin' Stevens (1981)
YOUNG LOVE Tab Hunter (1957) and
   Donny Osmond (1973)

GEORGE HARRISON'S TOP 40

On January 1, 1966, Tony Hall's column in *Record Mirror* had a short piece about the juke-box (a KB) that Beatle George Harrison had in the den of his Esher home, and which was also featured briefly in the film *Help!*

George was quoted: "It's so much easier to have all my favourite records on the juke-box at once. It saves me going through piles of records to find the ones I want. Then, when I get sick of them, I just throw them out and put some new ones in."

Tony then went on to list George's current 40 favourite sounds, as follows:

1 HARLEM SHUFFLE Bob And Earl ★
2 GOOD THINGS COME TO THOSE WHO WAIT
   Chuck Jackson
3 BE MY LADY/RED BEANS AND RICE
   Booker T & The MGs
4 CAN YOU PLEASE CRAWL OUT YOUR WINDOW
   Bob Dylan
5 BABY, YOU'RE MY EVERYTHING
   Little Jerry Williams
6 BACK STREET Edwin Starr
7 WORK, WORK, WORK Lee Dorsey
8 THE LITTLE GIRL I ONCE KNEW Beach Boys
9 MY GIRL HAS GONE Miracles
10 I DON'T KNOW WHAT YOU'VE GOT,
   BUT IT'S GOT ME (Part 2) Little Richard
11 I CAN'T TURN YOU LOOSE Otis Redding
12 MY GIRL Otis Redding
13 I BELIEVE I'LL LOVE ON Jackie Wilson
14 PLUM NELLIE Booker T & The MGs
15 EVERYTHING IS GONNA BE ALRIGHT
   Willie Mitchell
16 A SWEET WOMAN LIKE YOU Joe Tex
17 SOMETHING ABOUT YOU Four Tops
18 I GOT YOU (I FEEL GOOD) James Brown
19 AIN'T THAT PECULIAR Marvin Gaye

20 TURN! TURN! TURN! Byrds
21 SEE SAW Don Covay
22 I'M COMIN' THROUGH Sounds Incorporated
23 DON'T FIGHT IT Wilson Pickett
24 BOOT-LEG Booker T & The MGs
25 I AIN'T GONNA EAT OUT MY HEART ANYMORE
   Young Rascals
26 RESPECT Otis Redding
27 TRY ME/PAPA'S GOT A BRAND NEW BAG
   (Instrumental Versions) James Brown
28 I'VE BEEN LOVING YOU TOO LONG Otis Redding
29 ALL OR NOTHING Patti LaBelle & Her Belles
30 PRETTY LITTLE BABY Marvin Gaye
31 OO WEE BABY, I LOVE YOU Fred Hughes
32 THE TRACKS OF MY TEARS Miracles
33 YUM YUM Joe Tex
34 AGENT OO-SOUL Edwin Starr
35 MONEY Barrett Strong
36 SOME OTHER GUY Ritchie Barrett
37 IT WASN'T ME Chuck Berry
38 MOHAIR SAM Charlie Rich
39 LET HIM RUN WILD Beach Boys
   (flip of CALIFORNIA GIRLS)
40 DO YOU BELIEVE IN
   MAGIC Lovin' Spoonful

Bear in mind that, with the
exception of a few "revived 45s",
this was basically a chart of
current favourites. As such, it
certainly shows how far the
Harrison head was into the
progressive (by British standards)
soul music of the day.

The singles by the Young Rascals and Lovin Spoonful were their début
American hits, and this was long before either group had a UK success.
Bob Dylan's 'Can You Please Crawl Out Your Window' was listed here
before it was available anywhere in the world; George had gotten hold of
an early mis-pressing of 'Positively 4th Street' where the wrong master
tape had been used!

ACTS WHO PLAYED THE 1969 ISLE OF WIGHT POP FESTIVAL

(AUGUST 29-31)

BOB DYLAN
THE BAND
THE WHO
MOODY BLUES
THE NICE
JOE COCKER &
  THE GREASE BAND
RICHIE HAVENS
BONZO DOG
  DOO-DAH BAND★
PRETTY THINGS
FAT MATTRESS
JULIE FELIX
MARSHA HUNT★
ECLECTION
THE THIRD EAR BAND
FAMILY
WHITE TRASH
AYNSLEY DUNBAR
BLODWYN PIG
(Featuring Multi-instrumentalist JACK LANCASTER)

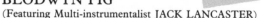

GYPSY
FREE
BLONDE ON BLONDE
EDGAR BROUGHTON
(Featuring GINGER MILLS)

KING CRIMSON
TOM PAXTON
THE PENTANGLE
GARY FARR
THE LIVERPOOL SCENE
INDO-JAZZ FUSIONS

SONGS FEATURED
BY BOB DYLAN ON HIS
ISLE OF WIGHT APPEARANCE

SHE BELONGS TO ME
I THREW IT ALL AWAY
MAGGIE'S FARM
WILD MOUNTAIN THYME
IT AIN'T ME, BABE
TO RAMONA
MR TAMBOURINE MAN
I DREAMED I SAW ST AUGUSTINE
LAY LADY LAY
HIGHWAY 61 REVISITED
ONE TOO MANY MORNINGS
I PITY THE POOR IMMIGRANT
LIKE A ROLLING STONE
I'LL BE YOUR BABY TONIGHT
THE MIGHTY QUINN

Encores:

MINSTREL BOY
RAINY DAY WOMEN, Nos. 12 & 35

Bob Dylan's Isle of Wight appearance with The Band (who also preceded him with their own act), was watched by some 200,000 people, including Beatles John Lennon, Ringo Starr and George Harrison, plus wives. The Fab Three zoomed in and out specifically to watch The Zim. Keith Richard; Bill Wyman and Charlie Watts from The Rolling Stones were also in the audience, as were Stevie Winwood and Jim Capaldi of Traffic.

THE ACTS WHO PLAYED THE 1970 ISLE OF WIGHT FESTIVAL

In approximate order of appearance . . .

Wednesday, August 26
REDBONE
MIGHTY BABY★
JUDAS JUMP
KATHY SMITH
(Wednesday was a warm-up "free day" for the festival proper)

Thursday, August 27
GROUNDHOGS
ANDY ROBERTS & EVERYONE
SUPERTRAMP
BLACK WIDOW
HOWL
TERRY REID

Friday, August 28
ARRIVAL
TASTE
CHICAGO
CACTUS
FAMILY
TONY JOE WHITE
LIGHTHOUSE
PROCOL HARUM
VOICES OF EAST HARLEM ✦
MELANIE

Saturday, August 29
JOHN SEBASTIAN (joined impromptu by
   ZAL YANOVSKY)
SHAWN PHILLIPS
EMERSON, LAKE & PALMER
TEN YEARS AFTER
DOORS ★
JONI MITCHELL
TINY TIM ★
MILES DAVIS
WHO
SLY & THE FAMILY STONE

Sunday, August 30
KRIS KRISTOFFERSON
RALPH McTELL
HEAVEN
FREE
DONOVAN
PENTANGLE
MOODY BLUES
JETHRO TULL ★
JIMI HENDRIX EXPERIENCE
JOAN BAEZ
RICHIE HAVENS
LEONARD COHEN with THE ARMY

Billed to appear but absent in the event were Cat Mother & The All-Night Newsboys, Spirit, The Everly Brothers and Mungo Jerry.

The festival made a hefty loss — tens of thousands of pounds — mainly due to loss of receipts from tickets after a sizeable yobbo element broke down the security fences and let thousands in for free. Also, 30 or 40 thousand people found that by camping on the hill overlooking the sight, they could hear the music perfectly, and so didn't bother making their way down to the stage front a quarter of a mile or so away.

THE NEW MUSICAL EXPRESS POLL-WINNERS

From almost the time of its inception in the early 1950s, the *NME* has had an annual readers' poll. The early years reflected the paper's original readership of musicians and songwriters; but once rock and roll had arrived, the *NME* quickly became a pop fans' weekly bible and the poll emphasis changed too, introducing categories which reflected the acts and records making the pop charts.

When the paper metamorphosed into a more serious rock weekly during the 1970s, the poll changed once again, reintroducing sections (similar to those which had existed in the early 50s) for players of individual instruments, and giving attention to acts in the rock album market. Further developments in popular musical taste have also been reflected by other changes and new categories in subsequent years, as the tables of winners appearing below illustrate.

BEST SINGLE OF THE YEAR

1959 LIVING DOLL Cliff Richard ★
1960 APACHE Shadows
1961 JOHNNY REMEMBER ME John Leyton
1962 I REMEMBER YOU Frank Ifield
1963 SHE LOVES YOU Beatles
1964 HOUSE OF THE RISING SUN Animals
1965 SATISFACTION Rolling Stones
1966 ELEANOR RIGBY Beatles
1967 A WHITER SHADE OF PALE Procol Harum ★

1968 HEY JUDE Beatles
1969 HONKY TONK WOMEN Rolling Stones
1970 IN THE SUMMERTIME Mungo Jerry
1971 MY SWEET LORD George Harrison
1972 SILVER MACHINE Hawkwind (UK)
     SCHOOL'S OUT Alice Cooper (World) ★

1973 5.15 Who (UK)
     RADAR LOVE Golden Earring (World)
1974 CAN'T GET ENOUGH Bad Company
1975 BOHEMIAN RHAPSODY Queen
1976 THE BOYS ARE BACK IN TOWN Thin Lizzy
1977 GOD SAVE THE QUEEN Sex Pistols
1978 (WHITE MAN) IN HAMMERSMITH PALAIS
     Clash
1979 GANGSTERS Specials
1980 GOING UNDERGROUND Jam
1981 GHOST TOWN Specials
1982 TOWN CALLED MALICE Jam

Until the early 1970s, voting in this category was restricted to British-recorded singles. In 1972 and 1973 there were separate polls for UK and world-wide releases, and subsequently there have been no restrictions – although in common with almost every *NME* poll category in recent years, the winners have been of British origin anyway.

ALBUM OF THE YEAR

1970 LET IT BE Beatles
1971 ELECTRIC WARRIOR T. Rex
1972 NEVER A DULL MOMENT Rod Stewart
1973 THE DARK SIDE OF THE MOON Pink Floyd
1974 SMILER Rod Stewart
1975 PHYSICAL GRAFFITI Led Zeppelin
1976 THE SONG REMAINS THE SAME Led Zeppelin
1977 NEVER MIND THE BOLLOCKS . . .
      HERE'S THE SEX PISTOLS Sex Pistols
1978 ALL MOD CONS Jam
1979 SETTING SONS Jam
1980 SOUND AFFECTS Jam
1981 HEAVEN UP HERE Echo & The Bunnymen
1982 THE GIFT Jam

Because of the extreme singles-orientated approach of the *NME* prior to 1970, there was no category for nominating a favourite album prior to this date.

WORLD VOCAL GROUP

1956 FOUR ACES
1957 PLATTERS
1958 EVERLY BROTHERS ★
1959 EVERLY BROTHERS
1960 EVERLY BROTHERS
1961 EVERLY BROTHERS
1962 EVERLY BROTHERS
1963 BEATLES
1964 BEATLES
1965 BEATLES
1966 BEACH BOYS
1967 BEATLES
1968 BEATLES
1969 BEATLES
1970 CREEDENCE CLEARWATER REVIVAL
1971 T. REX
1972 ALICE COOPER
1973 YES
1974 LED ZEPPELIN
1975 LED ZEPPELIN
1976 LED ZEPPELIN
1977 SEX PISTOLS
1978 CLASH
1979 JAM
1980 JAM
1981 JAM
1982 JAM

The category has been known simply as "group" in recent years.

WORLD MUSICAL PERSONALITY

1956 BILL HALEY
1957 ELVIS PRESLEY
1958 ELVIS PRESLEY
1959 ELVIS PRESLEY
1960 DUANE EDDY
1961 ELVIS PRESLEY
1962 ELVIS PRESLEY
1963 ELVIS PRESLEY
1964 ELVIS PRESLEY
1965 ELVIS PRESLEY
1966 ELVIS PRESLEY
1967 ELVIS PRESLEY
1968 ELVIS PRESLEY
1969 ELVIS PRESLEY
1970 ELVIS PRESLEY
1971 ELVIS PRESLEY

This category was discontinued after 1971.

WORLD MALE SINGER

1955 FRANK SINATRA ★
1956 FRANK SINATRA
1957 PAT BOONE
1958 ELVIS PRESLEY
1959 ELVIS PRESLEY
1960 ELVIS PRESLEY
1961 ELVIS PRESLEY
1962 ELVIS PRESLEY
1963 CLIFF RICHARD
1964 ELVIS PRESLEY
1965 ELVIS PRESLEY
1966 ELVIS PRESLEY
1967 ELVIS PRESLEY
1968 ELVIS PRESLEY
1969 ELVIS PRESLEY
1970 ELVIS PRESLEY
1971 ELVIS PRESLEY
1972 ELVIS PRESLEY

1973 DAVID BOWIE
1974 ROBERT PLANT
1975 ROBERT PLANT
1976 ROBERT PLANT
1977 DAVID BOWIE
1978 DAVID BOWIE
1979 STING
1980 PAUL WELLER
1981 DAVID BOWIE
1982 PAUL WELLER

WORLD FEMALE SINGER

1955 DORIS DAY
1956 DORIS DAY
1957 DORIS DAY
1958 CONNIE FRANCIS
1959 CONNIE FRANCIS
1960 CONNIE FRANCIS
1961 CONNIE FRANCIS
1962 BRENDA LEE
1963 BRENDA LEE
1964 BRENDA LEE
1965 DUSTY SPRINGFIELD
1966 DUSTY SPRINGFIELD
1967 DUSTY SPRINGFIELD
1968 LULU
1969 DUSTY SPRINGFIELD
1970 DIANA ROSS ★
1971 DIANA ROSS
1972 MAGGIE BELL
1973 DIANA ROSS
1974 JONI MITCHELL
1975 JONI MITCHELL
1976 LINDA RONSTADT
1977 JULIE COVINGTON
1978 DEBBIE HARRY
1979 KATE BUSH
1980 SIOUXSIE
1981 SIOUXSIE
1982 SIOUXSIE

UK VOCAL GROUP

1954 STARGAZERS
1955 STARGAZERS
1956 STARGAZERS
1957 KING BROTHERS
1958 MUDLARKS
1959 MUDLARKS
1960 KING BROTHERS
1961 SPRINGFIELDS ★

1962 SPRINGFIELDS
1963 BEATLES
1964 BEATLES
1965 BEATLES
1966 BEATLES
1967 BEATLES
1968 BEATLES
1969 BEATLES
1970 BEATLES
1971 T. REX
1972 SLADE
1973 YES
1974 ROXY MUSIC
1975 LED ZEPPELIN

After 1975, this section was combined with the world vocal group category – or, in effect, thrown open to all comers. Subsequent winners have all been British groups in any case.

UK MALE SINGER

1952 DICKIE VALENTINE
1953 DICKIE VALENTINE
1954 DICKIE VALENTINE
1955 DICKIE VALENTINE
1956 DICKIE VALENTINE
1957 DICKIE VALENTINE
1958 FRANKIE VAUGHAN
1959 CLIFF RICHARD
1960 CLIFF RICHARD
1961 CLIFF RICHARD
1962 CLIFF RICHARD
1963 CLIFF RICHARD
1964 CLIFF RICHARD
1965 CLIFF RICHARD
1966 CLIFF RICHARD
1967 TOM JONES
1968 TOM JONES
1969 TOM JONES
1970 CLIFF RICHARD
1971 CLIFF RICHARD
1972 ROD STEWART
1973 DAVID BOWIE
1974 PAUL RODGERS
1975 ROBERT PLANT ★

As with the UK vocal group section, this category was combined with its world-wide equivalent into an all-comers poll after 1975.

UK FEMALE SINGER

1952 LITA ROZA
1953 LITA ROZA
1954 LITA ROZA
1955 RUBY MURRAY
1956 ALMA COGAN
1957 ALMA COGAN
1958 ALMA COGAN
1959 SHIRLEY BASSEY
1960 SHIRLEY BASSEY
1961 HELEN SHAPIRO ★
1962 HELEN SHAPIRO
1963 KATHY KIRBY
1964 DUSTY SPRINGFIELD ★
1965 DUSTY SPRINGFIELD
1966 DUSTY SPRINGFIELD
1967 LULU
1968 LULU
1969 LULU
1970 CILLA BLACK
1971 CILLA BLACK
1972 MAGGIE BELL
1973 MAGGIE BELL
1974 KIKI DEE
1975 KIKI DEE

As with the vocal group and male singer sections, this category was effectively combined with its world-wide equivalent after 1975.

UK VOCAL PERSONALITY

1955 DICKIE VALENTINE
1956 (No award given)
1957 TOMMY STEELE
1958 FRANKIE VAUGHAN
1959 FRANKIE VAUGHAN
1960 LONNIE DONEGAN ★
1961 ADAM FAITH
1962 JOE BROWN
1963 JOE BROWN
1964 CLIFF RICHARD
1965 JOHN LENNON
1966 CLIFF RICHARD
1967 CLIFF RICHARD
1968 CLIFF RICHARD
1969 CLIFF RICHARD
1970 CLIFF RICHARD
1971 CLIFF RICHARD

Like its world-wide equivalent, this category was discontinued after 1971.

NEW DISC OR TV SINGER

1958 CLIFF RICHARD
1959 CRAIG DOUGLAS
1960 EMILE FORD
1961 JOHN LEYTON
1962 FRANK IFIELD
1963 GERRY MARSDEN
1964 MICK JAGGER
1965 DONOVAN
1966 STEVIE WINWOOD
1967 ENGELBERT HUMPERDINCK★
1968 MARY HOPKIN
1969 CLODAGH RODGERS
1970 ELTON JOHN
1971 ROD STEWART

This category was discontinued after 1971.

BEST NEW GROUP/
MOST PROMISING ARTIST

1964 ROLLING STONES
1965 SEEKERS
1966 SPENCER DAVIS
1967 BEE GEES
1968 LOVE AFFAIR
1969 JETHRO TULL
1970 McGUINNESS FLINT
1971 NEW SEEKERS
1972 ROXY MUSIC (UK)
     FOCUS (World)
1973 LEO SAYER (UK)
     GOLDEN EARRING (World)
1974 BAD COMPANY
1975 BE BOP DELUXE (UK)
     BRUCE SPRINGSTEEN (World)
1976 EDDIE & THE HOT RODS
1977 TOM ROBINSON
1978 PUBLIC IMAGE LIMITED
1979 SPECIALS
1980 UB40
1981 ALTERED
     IMAGES
1982 No category

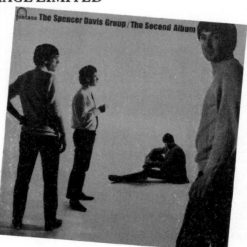

Like several other poll categories, the best newcomer was originally only open to UK artists; it was then split into two sections in the early 1970s and subsequently thrown wide open — with Britishers winning in any case.

STAGE BAND/LIVE ACT

1972 SLADE
1973 ALICE COOPER★
1974 GENESIS (UK)
     PINK FLOYD (World)
1975 QUEEN (UK)
     WHO (World)
1982 JAM

UK MALE DANCE BAND VOCALIST

1955 BOBBIE BRITTON

UK FEMALE DANCE BAND VOCALIST

1955 ROSE BRENNAN

FILM

1978 CLOSE ENCOUNTERS OF THE THIRD KIND
1979 QUADROPHENIA
1980 THE ELEPHANT MAN
1981 GREGORY'S GIRL
1982 E.T. – THE EXTRA TERRESTRIAL

ARTIST FOR POLL CONCERT

During this period, readers were invited to nominate the act they would most like to see appearing in the live poll-winners concert, sponsored by the *NME*. The concert took place in London a few months after the year's results were published.

1959 MARTY WILDE
1960 ADAM FAITH
1961 BILLY FURY
1962 BILLY FURY
1963 BILLY J. KRAMER & THE DAKOTAS

TRAD JAZZ BAND

1961 ACKER BILK
1962 KENNY BALL
1963 KENNY BALL

UK BLUES/
R'n'B GROUP

1964 ROLLING STONES ★
1965 ROLLING STONES
1966 ROLLING STONES
1967 ROLLING STONES
1968 ROLLING STONES
1969 FLEETWOOD MAC

Both of the above categories were introduced in response to strong musical trends of the time. Once the genres had run out of commercial steam, and/or been absorbed back into the mainstream, they vanished again from the poll.

GUITAR

1953 IVOR MAIRANTS
1954 BERT WEEDON

1972 ERIC CLAPTON (UK) ★
      ERIC CLAPTON (World)
1973 ERIC CLAPTON
1974 ERIC CLAPTON
1975 JIMMY PAGE
1976 JIMMY PAGE
1977 JIMMY PAGE
1978 MICK JONES
1979 PAUL WELLER
1980 PAUL WELLER
1981 PAUL WELLER
1982 PAUL WELLER

BASS

1953 JOHNNY HAWKSWORTH
1954 JOHNNY HAWKSWORTH

1972 PAUL McCARTNEY (UK) ★
     PAUL McCARTNEY (World)
1973 PAUL McCARTNEY
1974 PAUL McCARTNEY
1975 CHRIS SQUIRE
1976 PAUL McCARTNEY
1977 JEAN JACQUES BURNEL
1978 BRUCE FOXTON ★
1979 BRUCE FOXTON
1980 BRUCE FOXTON
1981 BRUCE FOXTON
1982 BRUCE FOXTON

PIANO/KEYBOARDS

1953 BILL McGUFFIE
1954 BILL McGUFFIE

1972 KEITH EMERSON
1973 RICK WAKEMAN ★
1974 RICK WAKEMAN
1975 RICK WAKEMAN
1976 RICK WAKEMAN
1977 RICK WAKEMAN
1978 DAVE GREENFIELD
1979 DAVE GREENFIELD
1980 DAVE GREENFIELD
1981 DAVE GREENFIELD
1982 No category

DRUMS

1953 JACK PARNELL
1954 RONNIE VERRELL

1972 CARL PALMER
1973 CARL PALMER
1974 CARL PALMER
1975 KEITH MOON
1976 JOHN BONHAM
1977 PAUL COOK
1978 KEITH MOON
1979 RICK BUCKLER
1980 RICK BUCKLER
1981 RICK BUCKLER
1982 RICK BUCKLER

CLARINET

1954 VIC ASH

BARITONE SAX

1954 HARRY KLEIN

TROMBONE

1954 DON LUSHER

VIBRAPHONE

1954 VICTOR FELDMAN

ALTO SAXOPHONE

1953 JOHN DANKWORTH
1954 JOHN DANKWORTH

TENOR SAX

1953 RONNIE SCOTT
1954 TOMMY WHITTLE

TRUMPET

1953 KENNY BAKER
1954 KENNY BAKER

ELECTRONICS

1982 VINCE CLARKE

OTHER INSTRUMENT

1980 SAXA (Saxophone)
1982 EMERALD EXPRESS (Violin)

LARGE BAND/ORCHESTRA

1952 TED HEATH
1953 TED HEATH
1954 TED HEATH
1955 TED HEATH
1956 TED HEATH
1957 TED HEATH
1958 TED HEATH
1959 TED HEATH
1960 TED HEATH
1961 TED HEATH
1962 JOE LOSS
1963 JOE LOSS

MOST PROMISING NEWCOMER

1955 RONNIE SCOTT

SOLO INSTRUMENTALIST/ INSTRUMENTAL PERSONALITY

1952 RONNIE SCOTT
1953 RONNIE SCOTT
1954 ERIC DELANEY
1955 EDDIE CALVERT

1958 EDDIE CALVERT
1959 RUSS CONWAY
1960 RUSS CONWAY
1961 BERT WEEDON
1962 JET HARRIS
1963 JET HARRIS

1972 IAN ANDERSON (UK)
     KEITH EMERSON (World)
1973 ROY WOOD
1974 MIKE OLDFIELD ★
1975 MIKE OLDFIELD
1976 MIKE OLDFIELD
1977 MIKE OLDFIELD

DISC JOCKEY

1956 JACK JACKSON
1957 JACK JACKSON
1958 JACK JACKSON/PETE MURRAY (tied)
1959 PETE MURRAY
1960 DAVID JACOBS
1961 DAVID JACOBS
1962 DAVID JACOBS
1963 DAVID JACOBS
1964 JIMMY SAVILE
1965 JIMMY SAVILE
1966 JIMMY SAVILE
1967 JIMMY SAVILE
1968 JIMMY SAVILE
1969 JIMMY SAVILE
1970 JIMMY SAVILE
1971 JIMMY SAVILE
1972 JOHN PEEL ★
1973 JOHN PEEL
1974 NOEL EDMONDS
1975 JOHN PEEL
1976 JOHN PEEL
1977 JOHN PEEL
1978 JOHN PEEL
1979 JOHN PEEL
1980 JOHN PEEL
1981 JOHN PEEL
1982 No category

For many years this category was only open to UK-based DJs, though in recent years it has theoretically been available to all comers. Yet, despite that, of all those categories which have had long continuous runs in the poll, it is the one with the fewest different winners. It may be because the paper was affeared of John Peel copping the title yet again during 1982, that the section was discontinued that year.

BEST TV SHOW

1964 READY STEADY GO!
1965 TOP OF THE POPS ★
1966 TOP OF THE POPS
1967 TOP OF THE POPS
1968 TOP OF THE POPS
1969 TOP OF THE POPS
1970 TOP OF THE POPS
1971 TOP OF THE POPS
1972 THE OLD GREY WHISTLE TEST
1973 THE OLD GREY WHISTLE TEST
1974 THE OLD GREY WHISTLE TEST
1975 THE OLD GREY WHISTLE TEST
1976 THE OLD GREY WHISTLE TEST
1977 THE OLD GREY WHISTLE TEST
1978 REVOLVER
1979 FAWLTY TOWERS
1980 NOT THE NINE O'CLOCK NEWS
1981 CORONATION STREET
1982 THE YOUNG ONES

BEST RADIO SHOW

1972 SOUND OF THE 70S
1973 SOUND OF THE 70S
1974 ALAN FREEMAN SHOW
1975 ALAN FREEMAN SHOW
1976 ALAN FREEMAN'S SATURDAY SHOW
1977 JOHN PEEL SHOW
1978 JOHN PEEL SHOW
1979 JOHN PEEL SHOW
1980 No category
1981 JOHN PEEL SHOW
1982 JOHN PEEL SHOW

MOST ENTERPRISING LABEL

1972 ISLAND (UK)
RCA (World)

It is interesting to speculate
why this category only
appeared for one year.
Mutters from other
labels which advertised
in the paper, perhaps?

PRODUCER

1972 GREG LAKE
1973 DAVID BOWIE
1974 EDDIE OFFORD
1975 JIMMY PAGE

MOST OVERRATED SINGLE OF THE YEAR

1972 MOULDY OLD DOUGH Lieutenant Pigeon (UK)
     PUPPY LOVE Donny Osmond (World)
1973 TIE A YELLOW RIBBON ROUND THE OLD
     OAK TREE Tony Orlando & Dawn
1974 KUNG FU FIGHTING Carl Douglas

Overrated by whom, one wonders? All of the above came in for plenty of critical knocks at the time they were hits. Perhaps the ambiguity of the category caused its early demise from the poll.

ARRANGER

1953 REG OWEN
1954 REG OWEN

IMAGE OF THE YEAR

1979 GARY NUMAN

FACE OF THE DECADE

1979 JOHNNY ROTTEN ★

FARCE OF THE DECADE

1979 MOD REVIVAL

HAIRCUT OF THE YEAR

1980 EUGENE REYNOLDS
1982 PAUL WELLER

DANCEFLOOR RECORD

1982 YOUNG GUNS (GO FOR IT) Wham!

BEST DRESSED PERSON

1980 ADAM ANT
1981 MICHAEL FOOT
1982 PAUL WELLER (Male)
      SIOUXSIE (Female)

PROMO VIDEO

1982 HOUSE OF FUN Madness

JAZZ ACT

1975 WEATHER REPORT

COUNTRY ACT

1975 EAGLES

FOLK ACT

1975 STEELEYE SPAN

SOUL ACT

1973 STEVIE WONDER★
1974 STEVIE WONDER
1975 BOB MARLEY

EVENT OF THE YEAR

1977　THE DEATH OF ELVIS PRESLEY
1980　THE DEATH OF JOHN LENNON
1982　JAM SPLIT

MOST MISSED DEAD ACT

1976　JIMI HENDRIX

MOST WONDERFUL HUMAN BEING

1976　JOHNNY ROTTEN
1977　JOHNNY ROTTEN
1978　SID VICIOUS
1979　JOHN PEEL
1980　PAUL WELLER
1981　PAUL WELLER
1982　PAUL WELLER

BEST DRESSED LP

1973 YESSONGS Yes
1974 RELAYER Yes
1975 PHYSICAL GRAFFITI Led Zeppelin
1976 THE SONG REMAINS THE SAME Led Zeppelin
1977 NEVER MIND THE BOLLOCKS . . .
       HERE'S THE SEX PISTOLS Sex Pistols
1978 SOME GIRLS Rolling Stones
1979 METAL BOX Public Image Limited
1980 SOUND AFFECTS Jam
1981 HEAVEN UP HERE Echo & The Bunnymen
1982 A KISS IN THE DREAMHOUSE
       Siouxsie & The Banshees

SONGWRITERS

1973 ELTON JOHN/
       BERNIE TAUPIN
1976 BOB DYLAN
1977 DAVID BOWIE
1978 ELVIS COSTELLO
1979 PAUL WELLER ★
1980 PAUL WELLER
1981 PAUL WELLER
1982 PAUL WELLER

KLUTZ/TURKEY/PRAT OR CREEP OF THE YEAR

1974 STEVE HARLEY
1975 BAY CITY ROLLERS
1976 SEX PISTOLS
1977 FREDDIE MERCURY
1978 JOHN TRAVOLTA ★
1979 GARY NUMAN
1980 MARGARET THATCHER
1981 ADAM ANT
1982 MARGARET THATCHER

PIN UP

1978

DEBBIE HARRY

THE 'ROLLING STONE' ANNUAL MUSIC POLLS

THE READERS' POLL

BEST ARTIST	THE CRITICS' POLL
1976 PETER FRAMPTON	PAUL McCARTNEY
1977 FLEETWOOD MAC	(No award given)
1978 BRUCE SPRINGSTEEN	ROLLING STONES
1979 NEIL YOUNG	WHO
WHO	
1980 BRUCE SPRINGSTEEN	BRUCE SPRINGSTEEN ★
1981 ROLLING STONES	ROLLING STONES
1982 BRUCE SPRINGSTEEN	PRINCE

BEST BAND

1976	WHO	FLEETWOOD MAC
1977	FLEETWOOD MAC	FLEETWOOD MAC
1978	ROLLING STONES	BRUCE SPRINGSTEEN & THE E STREET BAND
1979	WHO	WHO
1980	E STREET BAND	CLASH
1981	ROLLING STONES	POLICE
1982	CLASH	CLASH ★

BEST MALE VOCALIST

1976 PAUL McCARTNEY   (No award given)
1977 JAMES TAYLOR   (No award given)
1978 BRUCE SPRINGSTEEN   BOB SEGER
1979 NEIL YOUNG ★   VAN MORRISON
1980 BRUCE SPRINGSTEEN   WILLY DeVILLE
                                    JOHN LYDON
1981 MICK JAGGER   MICK JAGGER
                                    STING
1982 BRUCE SPRINGSTEEN   MICHAEL JACKSON

FEMALE VOCALIST

1976	LINDA RONSTADT	(No award given)
1977	LINDA RONSTADT	(No award given)
1978	LINDA RONSTADT	NICOLETTE LARSON
1979	DEBORAH HARRY	RICKIE LEE JONES
	RICKIE LEE JONES	
1980	PAT BENATAR ★	CHRISSIE HYNDE
1981	PAT BENATAR	RICKIE LEE JONES
	STEVIE NICKS	
1982	PAT BENATAR	LINDA THOMPSON

BEST ALBUM

1976	PETER FRAMPTON 'FRAMPTON COMES ALIVE!'	STEVE MILLER BAND 'FLY LIKE AN EAGLE'

1976 PETER FRAMPTON
    'FRAMPTON COMES ALIVE!'
1977 FLEETWOOD MAC
    'RUMOURS'

1978 ROLLING STONES
    'SOME GIRLS'
1979 NEIL YOUNG
    'RUST NEVER SLEEPS'
1980 BRUCE SPRINGSTEEN
    'THE RIVER'
1981 ROLLING STONES
    'TATTOO YOU'
1982 BRUCE SPRINGSTEEN
    'NEBRASKA'

STEVE MILLER BAND
    'FLY LIKE AN EAGLE'
SEX PISTOLS
    'NEVER MIND THE BOLLOCKS
    – HERE'S THE SEX PISTOLS'
ROLLING STONES
    'SOME GIRLS'
NEIL YOUNG
    'RUST NEVER SLEEPS'
CLASH 'LONDON CALLING'

ROLLING STONES
    'TATTOO YOU'
BRUCE SPRINGSTEEN
    'NEBRASKA'
RICHARD & LINDA THOMPSON
    'SHOOT OUT THE LIGHTS'

BEST SINGLE

1976 BLUE OYSTER CULT ★
    '(DON'T FEAR) THE REAPER'
1977 FLEETWOOD MAC
    'DREAMS'
1978 ROLLING STONES
    'MISS YOU'
1979 KNACK 'MY SHARONA'
1980 BRUCE SPRINGSTEEN
    'HUNGRY HEART'
1981 ROLLING STONES
    'START ME UP'
1982 CLASH 'ROCK THE CASBAH'

ROD STEWART
    'TONIGHT'S THE NIGHT'
BOB SEGER
    'NIGHT MOVES'
BEE GEES
    'STAYIN' ALIVE'
FLEETWOOD MAC 'TUSK'
JOY DIVISION
    'LOVE WILL TEAR US APART'
ROLLING STONES
    'START ME UP'
GRANDMASTER FLASH
    'THE MESSAGE'

BEST NEW ARTIST

1976 BOSTON	GRAHAM PARKER & THE RUMOUR
1977 FOREIGNER	PETER GABRIEL
	VALERIE CARTER
	TALKING HEADS
	GARLAND JEFFREYS
1978 CARS	CARS
1979 KNACK	POLICE ★
1980 PRETENDERS	PRETENDERS
1981 GO-GO'S	GO-GO'S
1982 MEN AT WORK ★	MARSHALL CRENSHAW ★

BEST SOUL ARTIST

Year	Winner	Runner-up
1976	STEVIE WONDER	(No award given)
1977	STEVIE WONDER	(No award given)
1978	COMMODORES	(No award given)
1979	EARTH, WIND & FIRE	DONNA SUMMER
1980	STEVIE WONDER	SMOKEY ROBINSON
1981	RICK JAMES	GRANDMASTER FLASH
1982	STEVIE WONDER ✦	PRINCE

BEST JAZZ ARTIST

1976 GEORGE BENSON   STANLEY CLARKE
1977 GEORGE BENSON   ORNETTE COLEMAN
1978 CHUCK MANGIONE   CHARLES MINGUS
1979 CHUCK MANGIONE   ART ENSEMBLE OF CHICAGO
1980 GEORGE BENSON   ARTHUR BLYTHE
1981 AL JARREAU   JAMES BLOOD ULMER
     GEORGE BENSON
1982 PAT METHENY   ORNETTE COLEMAN

BEST COUNTRY ARTIST

1976 WAYLON JENNINGS   GEORGE JONES
1977 DOLLY PARTON   DOLLY PARTON ★
1978 DOLLY PARTON   WILLIE NELSON
1979 CHARLIE DANIELS   WAYLON JENNINGS ★
     WILLIE NELSON
1980 WILLIE NELSON   BOBBY BARE
1981 WILLIE NELSON   JOHN ANDERSON
                            ROSANNE CASH
1982 WILLIE NELSON   RICKY SKAGGS

145

BEST PRODUCER

1976 (No award given)	TOM DOWD
1977 PETER ASHER	PETER ASHER
1978 PETER ASHER	BEE GEES, ALBHY
	GALUTEN & KARL RICHARDSON
1979 NICK LOWE	NICK LOWE ★
1980 JON LANDAU	CHRIS THOMAS
1981 JIMMY IOVINE	STEVE LILLYWHITE
1982 GEORGE MARTIN ★	MARTIN RUSHENT

BEST SONGWRITER

1976	(No award given)	(No award given)
1977	JACKSON BROWNE	(No award given)
1978	BRUCE SPRINGSTEEN	WARREN ZEVON
1979	NEIL YOUNG	ELVIS COSTELLO
1980	BRUCE SPRINGSTEEN	WALTER BECKER AND DONALD FAGEN JOE STRUMMER AND MICK JONES
1981	MICK JAGGER AND KEITH RICHARDS	CHRIS DIFFORD AND GLENN TILBROOK ★
1982	BRUCE SPRINGSTEEN	ELVIS COSTELLO

Although *Rolling Stone* magazine was launched in the late 1960s, quickly becoming America's leading rock music publication, it was not until the mid-1970s that they invited feedback from readers in the form of annual polls. The first such poll appeared in 1976, and they have continued to the present day in tandem with a "Critics' Poll" (in which contributors to the magazine and other recognised commentators on the rock scene are asked to cast their own votes in the same categories voted for by readers). The two separate sets of results, published together, show interesting comparisons of popular and critical taste – some unexpected corrolations as well as extreme divergencies.

Comparison of the *Rolling Stone* winners with those in similar categories of the British *NME* polls for the same years (also in this book) tends to underline the increasing divergence of musical tastes and attitudes on the two sides of the Atlantic after the 60s and early 70s.

'THE ROCK MARKETPLACE' TRIVIA POLLS

During 1974, the American magazine *The Rock Marketplace* conducted a readers' poll which offered categories a little more esoteric and wide-ranging than those found in the large publications. Some interesting results were polled, and below are some of the results under less familiar categories. To keep it in historical perspective, bear in mind that the poll was conducted during the early-mid 1970s amongst a readership for whom 60s nostalgia was still particularly strong.

FAVOURITE ALL-TIME LIVE ACT

1 THE WHO ★
2 ROLLING STONES
3 BEATLES
4 Beach Boys
5 Kinks
6 Stooges ★
7 Byrds
8 Jimi Hendrix
9 Alice Cooper
10 Yardbirds

FAVOURITE PRODUCER

1 Phil Spector
2 Brian Wilson ★
3 Tony Visconti
4 George Martin
5 Todd Rundgren
6 Jimmy Miller
7 Glyn Johns
8 Roy Wood
9 David Bowie
10 Shel Talmy

ACT READERS MOST WANT TO SEE LIVE

1 BEATLES
2 VELVET UNDERGROUND
3 ROLLING STONES
4 Creation ★
5 Move
6 Stooges
7 Hollies
8 Small Faces
9 MC5
10 Sweet

FAVOURITE VOCALIST OF ALL TIME

1 Paul McCartney
2 John Lennon
3 Paul Rodgers
4 Roger Daltrey
5 Mick Jagger
6 Ray Davies
7 Steve Marriott
8 Robert Plant
9 Colin Blunstone
10 Iggy Pop ★
10 Brian Wilson
10 Lou Reed

WOULD YOU PREFER TO HAVE LUNCH WITH LYNSEY DE PAUL, THE NEW YORK DOLLS OR SPARKS?

1 Lynsey De Paul ★
2 Sparks
3 New York Dolls

Almost 12% of the voters indicated that they would prefer to eat alone, and a further 12% said they would go hungry that day!

THE GREATEST ROCK 'N' ROLL BAND EVER?

1	ELVIS PRESLEY, SCOTTY MOORE, BILL BLACK AND D.J. FONTANA	32%
2	JERRY LEE LEWIS AND THE MEMPHIS BEAT	10%
3	BUDDY HOLLY AND THE CRICKETS	9%
4	BILL HALEY AND HIS COMETS	8.2%
5	GENE VINCENT AND THE BLUE CAPS	5.7%
6	SCREAMING LORD SUTCH AND THE SAVAGES	5%
7	ROLLING STONES	4.1%
8	BEATLES	3.3%
8	ASSOCIATION ★	3.3%
8	WILD ANGELS	3.3%
11	BAND/RONNIE HAWKINS' HAWKS	2.5%
11	LITTLE RICHARD AND HIS BAND	2.5%
13	JOHNNY BURNETTE TRIO	1.6%
13	SHAKIN' STEVENS AND THE SUNSETS	1.6%

This remarkable listing represents the results of a poll conducted by Charlie Gillett, author of the rock & roll history *Sound Of The City*, amongst readers of his "Echoes" column in the British music paper *Record Mirror*, during 1970. The poll was occasioned by the fact that The Rolling Stones at the time were being billed on their live shows as "The Greatest Rock & Roll Band In The World". Were they? asked Charlie — and if not, who *did* readers consider to be the all-time greatest rock & roll aggregation?

A loose definition of what constituted a group was allowed, and readers were also left to put their own interpretations on the phrase "rock & roll". Even so, there are some eyebrow-raisers, notably The Association tying in eighth position with The Beatles and The Wild Angels (the latter being Britain's most popular revivalists of traditional R&R at the time). Interesting, too, to see the then virtually unknown Shakin' Stevens and The Sunsets weighing in at joint 13th position. A mere eleven years later, Stevens was a British superstar, though still performing in an essentially 1950s-styled rock groove.

The percentage figures on the right-hand side represent the percentage of the total vote cast which was received by each act.

NME READERS' FAVOURITE ROCK VIDEOS OF 1982

As part of their readers' poll at the end of 1982, the *NME* introduced a new category asking voters to rank their favourite rock promotional video seen during the year. These were the ten which gained the most votes:

1 HOUSE OF FUN Madness ★
2 BUFFALO GALS Malcolm McLaren
3 THE BITTEREST PILL (I EVER HAD TO SWALLOW) Jam
4 ROCK THE CASBAH Clash
5 POISON ARROW ABC
6 OUR HOUSE Madness
7 PASS THE DUTCHIE Musical Youth
8 GOLDEN BROWN Stranglers ★
9 SHOCK THE MONKEY Peter Gabriel
10 RIO Duran Duran

All of these, note, are British acts. There were plenty of American videos showing on British TV, and the paper did not ask for votes to be restricted to domestic acts, so possibly something of a partisan attitude among *NME* readers is being reflected here.

THE MOST MISSED PERSON?

As part of its readers' poll in 1981, the *New Musical Express* asked voters to nominate the person whose absence from the scene they felt most acutely. Most took this (as the *NME* presumably intended) to mean rock stars who had died — not everyone thought so, however, as some of this list of the top 15 names reveals.

1 JOHN LENNON ★
2 IAN CURTIS (Joy Division)
3 BOB MARLEY ★
4 MALCOLM OWEN (Ruts)
5 MARC BOLAN ★
6 JIMI HENDRIX
7 JIM MORRISON
8 PETER SELLERS
9 NATALIE WOOD
10 BILL SHANKLY (uhh?)
11 KEITH MOON
12 SID VICIOUS
13 DAVID BOWIE (ha ha)
14 JOHN BONHAM
15 HOWARD DEVOTO

AMERICAN BANDSTAND'S GREATEST ALL-STAR ROCK BAND OF ALL TIME

As part of its celebratory 30th birthday show, Dick Clark's US *American Bandstand* TV pop showcase programme put together an all-star band of invited guests to play together on a standard rock number, Bill Haley's 'Rock Around The Clock'. They came from diverse branches of popular music, and almost every player was a star name in his own right, or part of a top-rated group. The result, perhaps surprisingly, was a solidly rocking and remarkably effective performance, which gave everybody space for a brief solo before letting them jam away in extended choruses.

There were no vocalists; *Bandstand* inserted vocal refrains by cutting an actual piece of film of Bill Haley singing his greatest hit into the instrumental jam at precisely the right points. The whole thing could have been utterly embarrassing, but it worked both musically and in TV terms. For that reason, it is worth preserving the names of the artists who played together in the remarkable one-off event. This was the line-up:

BO DIDDLEY (guitar)
DUANE EDDY (guitar)
AL JARDINE (guitar)
RAY PARKER JR. (guitar)
LEE RITENOUR (guitar)
JOHNNY RIVERS (guitar) ★
GEORGE THOROGOOD (guitar)
STANLEY CLARKE (bass)
LARRY GRAHAM (bass)
JAMES WILLIAM GUERCIO (bass)
DASH CROFTS (mandolin)
CHARLIE DANIELS (fiddle)
DOUG KERSHAW (fiddle)
MICK FLEETWOOD (drums)
NIGEL OLSSON (drums)
GEORGE DUKE (clavichord)
MICKEY GILLEY (piano)
BILLY PRESTON (organ)
FRANKIE AVALON (trumpet)
DONALD BYRD (trumpet)
BOOTS RANDOLPH (sax)
TOM SCOTT (sax)
JR. WALKER (sax)

ACTS WHO CHARTED ON THEIR OWN LABELS

BEATLES (Apple)
SPECIALS (2 Tone)
ABC (Neutron)
EDDY GRANT (Ice)
HERB ALPERT (A&M)
BEACH BOYS (Brother)
FRANK SINATRA (Reprise)
MOODY BLUES (Threshold)
JEFFERSON STARSHIP (Grunt)
JONATHAN KING (UK)★

There was a time when a certain level of consistent success in the pop world was marked by a familiar "status symbol" — that of the act opening up, and recording for, its own label. Motivations varied, but generally there was a feeling among the artists concerned that to have total creative freedom, and not to be answerable to someone else over musical or business decisions, would make for a generally better life.

In practice, it was rarely that straightforward. Acts would either get so involved manipulating the business side of their label that their music or internal relationships suffered, or they would be so heavily involved in the creative area that business and financial affairs ran riot.

Having suggested that, it must be added that Herb Alpert and Jerry Moss's A&M label has operated very successfully for upwards of 20 years now, while many of the others shown above very sensibly entered into licensing or distribution deals with larger record companies, thus un-shouldering some of their business worries whilst being able to concentrate on making music.

NOTABLY SUCCESSFUL NON-MOTOWN VERSIONS OF MOTOWN HITS

YOU CAN'T HURRY LOVE Phil Collins
  (originally The Supremes)
HE WAS REALLLY SAYIN' SOMETHIN'
  Bananarama (originally The Velvelettes)
THE TRACKS OF MY TEARS Linda Ronstadt ★
  (originally The Miracles)

YOU KEEP ME HANGIN' ON Vanilla Fudge
  (originally The Supremes)
TEARS OF A CLOWN The Beat
  (originally Smokey Robinson & The Miracles)
WHAT BECOMES OF THE BROKEN-HEARTED
  Dave Stewart with Colin Blunstone
  (originally Jimmy Ruffin)
MY GIRL Otis Redding (originally The Temptations)
I SECOND THAT EMOTION Japan
  (originally Smokey Robinson & The Miracles)
TOO BUSY THINKING ABOUT MY BABY
  Mardi Gras (originally Marvin Gaye)

I CAN'T HELP MYSELF Donnie Elbert
  (originally The Four Tops)
BABY I NEED YOUR LOVING Johnny Rivers
  (originally The Four Tops)
WHERE DID OUR LOVE GO Manhattan Transfer ★
  (originally The Supremes)
GOING TO A GO-GO Rolling Stones
  (originally The Miracles)
PLEASE MR POSTMAN Carpenters
  (originally The Marvelettes)
AIN'T NO MOUNTAIN HIGH ENOUGH
  Boys Town Gang (originally Diana Ross)
IT'S THE SAME OLD SONG
  KC & The Sunshine Band (originally The Four Tops)
AIN'T TOO PROUD TO BEG
  Rolling Stones (originally The Temptations)
YOU'RE ALL I NEED TO GET BY Aretha Franklin
  (originally Marvin Gaye & Tammi Terrell)
SHOP AROUND Captain & Temille
  (originally The Miracles)
REACH OUT, I'LL BE THERE Gloria Gaynor
  (originally The Four Tops)

Recent British revivals of Motown songs have been notable for doing better in the charts in this country than the original versions. Phil Collins climbed to No. 1 with 'You Can't Hurry Love', while The Supremes had only reached No. 3. Japan's No. 9 placing for 'I Second That Emotion' far outshadowed The Miracles' No. 27; and, while The Velvelettes' 'He Was Really Sayin' Somethin'' has never charted in the UK at all, Bananarama took the song to No. 5.

1983 HITS WHICH SHARE THEIR TITLES WITH HITS FROM THE PAST

Old songs are revived all the time, of course, and it is not at all infrequent for an oldie to enjoy a whole new lease of chart life in a revised form. Perhaps more interesting, though, is the revival of an old hit title to fit a brand-new song. The first half of 1983 saw such a flood of these songs that some observers were actually beginning to speculate whether every usable combination of English words had been tried out as a song title, and if we were now being forced to go back to the beginning again. Possibly, though, there has been a decided lack of imagination in songwriting ranks recently. In any event, all the following were sizeable hits on one side (or both) of the Atlantic, but their titles were not at all original.

1 BLUE MONDAY New Order (Fats Domino)
2 BREAKAWAY Tracey Ullman (Springfields)
3 CANDY GIRL New Edition (Four Seasons)
4 CANDY MAN Mary Jane Girls
   (Brian Poole & The Tremeloes)
5 COMMUNICATION BREAKDOWN Junior
   (Roy Orbison and Led Zeppelin — both different songs)
6 GARDEN PARTY Mezzoforte (Rick Nelson)
7 HEARTBREAKER Musical Youth (Dionne Warwick)
8 THE HOUSE THAT JACK BUILT Tracie
   (Alan Price and Aretha Franklin — both different songs)
9 I LIKE IT DeBarge (Gerry & The Pacemakers)
10 LET'S DANCE David Bowie (Chris Montez)

The names in brackets, of course, are the artists who were originally associated with these titles — but for different songs. It will be interesting to see how they all survive comparatively in ten years or so.

AROUND THE WORLD IN 80 ACTS . . .
being a round-up of ten acts from eight territories outside the US or UK, which managed to cross their chart success into the US or UK (or both) . . .

TEN JAMAICAN HIT-MAKERS

1 Prince Buster
2 Dennis Brown
3 Jimmy Cliff
4 Desmond Dekker
5 Bob Marley & The Wailers
6 Max Romeo
7 Barry Biggs
8 Dandy Livingstone
9 Dave & Ansil Collins
10 Upsetters

TEN DUTCH HIT-MAKERS

1 Focus
2 Pussy Cat
3 Golden Earring ★
4 Star Sound
5 Shocking Blue
6 George Baker Selection
7 Father Abraham & The Smurfs
8 Mouth And McNeal
9 Teach-In
10 Titanic

TEN CANADIAN HIT-MAKERS

1 Guess Who
2 Joni Mitchell
3 Neil Young
4 Gordon Lightfoot
5 Bachman-Turner Overdrive
6 Rush
7 Terry Jacks
8 Martha And The Muffins
9 Andy Kim
10 Patsy Gallant

TEN AUSTRALIAN HIT-MAKERS

1 Men At Work
2 AC/DC ★
3 Helen Reddy ★
4 Air Supply
5 Easybeats
6 Seekers
7 Samantha Sang
8 Rolf Harris
9 Sherbet
10 John Paul Young

TEN GERMAN HIT-MAKERS

1 Can
2 Kraftwerk ★
3 Scorpions
4 Rattles
5 Bert Kaempfert
6 Horst Jankowski
7 Munich Machine
8 Helmut Zacharius
9 Michael Schenker
10 Obernkirchen Children's Choir

TEN SCANDINAVIAN HIT-MAKERS

1 Abba ★
2 Spotnicks
3 Jorgen Ingman
4 Nina and Frederik
5 Hank C. Burnette
6 Sylvia (the Y VIVA ESPANA lady, not the
   PILLOW TALK one)
7 Harpo
8 Jan And Kjeld
9 Alice Babs
10 Stardust

TEN FRENCH HIT-MAKERS

1 Jean Michel Jarre ★
2 Charles Aznavour
3 Sheila (B Devotion)
4 Francoise Hardy
5 Patrick Juvet
6 Sacha Distel
7 Gilbert Becaud
8 Cerrone
9 Richard Anthony
10 La Belle Epoque

TEN ITALIAN HIT-MAKERS

1 Rene And Renato
2 Raffaella Cara
3 Gigliola Cinquetti
4 Emilio Pericoli
5 Marino Marini
6 Rita Pavone
7 Nini Rosso
8 Domenico Modugno
9 La Bionda
10 Marcello Minerbi

TEN ARTISTS WHO APPEARED IN A PRODUCTION OF THE MUSICAL 'HAIR'

MELBA MOORE
PAUL JABARA
DIANE KEATON
DOBIE GRAY
GLORIA JONES
MEAT LOAF ★
JENNIFER WARNES ★
BARRY McGUIRE
SONJA KRISTINA
PAUL NICHOLAS

Some of these (Dobie Gray, Barry McGuire) had already experienced commercial success on record before they played in 'Hair'. Most of the others have gone on to greater things since. Sonja Kristina (later with Curved Air) and Paul Nicholas were both in the successful first London production of the show, along with other artists like Marsha Hunt and J. Vincent Edwards.

TEN GROUPS FOR WHOM HAL BLAINE WAS THE DRUMMER YOU HEARD ON THE RECORD

1 ASSOCIATION
2 BEACH BOYS
3 BUCKINGHAMS
4 GARY LEWIS
  & THE PLAYBOYS
5 GRASS ROOTS
6 MAMAS & THE PAPAS ★
7 MONKEES
8 PARTRIDGE FAMILY
9 PAUL REVERE
  & THE RAIDERS
10 RONETTES

Hal Blaine is, and has been for over 25 years, the most active and in-demand session drummer on America's West Coast. The height of his playing fame came in the 1960s, when he could be heard tying down the beat on almost every hit record which came out of Los Angeles. Producers and record companies used him (and still do) because they could be sure of instant perfection behind the drumkit — regardless of whether the act being recorded ostensibly had its own drummer or not. Check out any of the big 1960s hits by the ten groups above, or almost any of the wealth of Phil Spector classics, (or even Elvis Presley's Hollywood-recorded movie songs), to discover just where you've been listening to Hal Blaine play for many years without realising it.

TEN ORIGINALS BY FRANKIE VALLI & THE FOUR SEASONS WHICH HAD HIT REVIVALS

The Four Seasons' catalogue has been more fruitful than most in providing material for later hit-makers. The songs marked with a * were originally Frankie Valli solo hits, and the rest were material recorded by the group. All songs were originally A-sides except 'Silence Is Golden', which was the flipside (for The Seasons) of 'Rag Doll'.

BEGGIN' Timebox
BYE BYE BABY (BABY GOODBYE) Bay City Rollers
CAN'T TAKE MY EYES OFF YOU★ Andy Williams
C'MON MARIANNE Grapefruit
LET'S HANG ON Barry Manilow ★
SHERRY Adrian Baker
SILENCE IS GOLDEN Tremeloes
THE PROUD ONE★ Osmonds
THE SUN AIN'T GONNA SHINE ANYMORE★
   Walker Brothers
WORKING MY WAY BACK TO YOU Detroit Spinners

THE CHICAGO AWARD FOR THE MOST BORING SEQUENCE OF TITLES

Readers of our first book in this series will appreciate the significance of the heading here (and we're not explaining it to the rest of you, because we'd like you to go and buy the other book!)

Chicago are still unchallenged in the boredom stakes because of the sheer volume of albums they have released. Although Peter Gabriel is doggedly trying to enter the same league, he has so far only released four albums all titled *Peter Gabriel* (all right, five if you count the alternative German-language version of one of them − we don't) − and that's only one more than Elvis Presley had called *Elvis*. Gabriel still has a long way to go.

So, in search of a variation on the theme, we scouted around for the most boring sequence of song titles to be found within the confines of *one* album. From plenty of yawn-inducing contenders, we chose the following array by Prince Far-1 because his album had more tracks on it than most of the other bores.

The album in question is *Psalms For I* by Prince Far-1

The tracks: **Psalm 49**
   Psalm 48
   Psalm 24
   Psalm 87
   The Lord's Prayer
   Psalm 95
   Psalm 53
   Psalm 23
   Psalm 2
   Psalm 1

Funny order, though, isn't it? And what a relief The Lord's Prayer brings . . .

ALISON MOYET (ALF of YAZOO)'S
ALL-TIME TEN FAVOURITE RECORDS

1 YOU'RE MY THRILL Billie Holiday ★
2 SUGAR SWEET Muddy Waters
3 SEX MACHINE James Brown
4 HOMOSAPIEN Pete Shelley
5 OUR LIPS ARE SEALED Fun Boy Three
6 KOSMIC BLUES Janis Joplin
7 CRAZY HE CALLS ME Billie Holiday
8 I NEED Buzzcocks
9 PALE SHELTER Tears For Fears
10 SHAME SHAME SHAME Irma Thomas

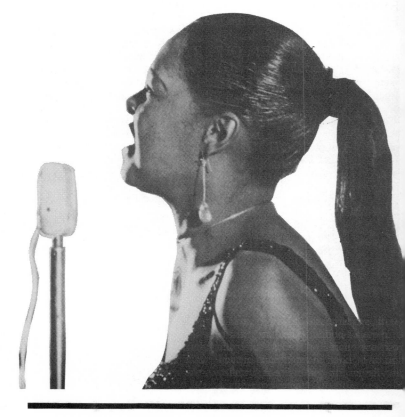

STUART COLMAN'S TEN FAVOURITE RECORDS BY ARTISTS WHO WEAR (OR WORE) SPECTACLES

RAY CHARLES Busted ★
BUDDY HOLLY Think It Over
STEVIE WONDER Boogie On Reggae Woman
GRAHAM PARKER Hotel Chambermaid
BO DIDDLEY Diddley Daddy
HANK MARVIN Throw Down A Line
ROY ORBISON Ooby Dooby
ELVIS COSTELLO Watching The Detectives ★
JOHN LENNON
Mind Games
ELTON JOHN
Honky Cat

BLANCMANGE'S NEIL ARTHUR'S TEN FAVOURITE STREET NAMES ★

INTACT ROAD
DUCKWORTH STREET
ALMOND STREET
STARKIE STREET
TOCHOLES ROAD
CRAVEN BROUFH
PUNSTOCK STREET
BOGHIGHT ROAD
HOLLINS GROVE STREET
SUNNYHURST LANE

BELLE STAR'S CLAIRE HURST'S TEN FAVOURITE THINGS

FUNKADELIC'S 'ELECTRIC SPANKING OF
  WAR BABIES'
SCOTCH & DRY
CORONATION STREET
MY SAXOPHONE
STILL LIFE WITH WOODPECKER – TOM ROBBINS
SUNDAY MORNINGS IN BED
BASIL'S THIGH
MILES DAVIS
HERMAN HESSE
SHRIEKBACK

GIRLSCHOOL'S KELLY JOHNSON'S FAVOURITE MISCELLANEOUS MUSICAL NOISES (NOT IN ORDER!)

1 THE THEME FROM 'STINGRAY'
2 ALMOST EVERYTHING BY BOWIE ★
3 THE YING TONG SONG Goons ★
4 DAVE GILMOUR'S GUITAR ON 'COMFORTABLY NUMB' (from THE WALL)
5 SCHOOL'S OUT Alice Cooper
6 BODIES Sex Pistols
7 SEE WHAT A FOOL I'VE BEEN Queen
8 VAN HALEN'S FIRST ALBUM
9 I SAY A LITTLE PRAYER Aretha Franklin ★
10 PLEASE DON'T TOUCH Motorhead and Girlschool

IN THE STRONGEST POSSIBLE TERMS
· · ·

In its July 1982 issue, the American record collectors' magazine, *Goldmine*, published an extensive chart of what were reckoned to be the all-time top protest songs. Most of them came from the 1960s, and most (but not all) were concerned with protest about war, the military, or aggression in general. This is the top 30 of that chart . . .

1 EVE OF DESTRUCTION Barry McGuire
2 IT'S GOOD NEWS WEEK
  Hedgehoppers Anonymous
3 WITH GOD ON OUR SIDE Manfred Mann ★
4 MASTERS OF WAR Bob Dylan
5 THE UNIVERSAL SOLDIER Donovan
6 BLOWIN' IN THE WIND Peter, Paul & Mary
7 SOCIETY'S CHILD Janis Ian
8 I AIN'T MARCHING ANYMORE Phil Ochs ★
9 FOR WHAT IT'S WORTH Buffalo Springfield
10 MORATORIUM Buffy Saint-Marie
11 THE WAR DRAGS ON Donovan
12 WE SHALL OVERCOME Joan Baez
13 THE WILLING CONSCRIPT Tom Paxton

Top songwriter amongst the above is obviously Bob Dylan, who wrote numbers 3, 4, 6 and 21. Also strongly represented are P.F. Sloan (numbers 1 and 18), and Buffy Saint-Marie (5 and 10).

50 WAYS TO LEAVE YOUR LOVER

1 ADIOS AMIGO Jim Reeves
2 AUF WEIDERSEH'N SWEETHEART Vera Lynn
3 BYE BYE BABY (BABY GOODBYE) Four Seasons
4 BYE BYE LOVE Everly Brothers
5 FAREWELL Rod Stewart
6 GET LOST Eden Kane
7 GET OFF MY BACK, WOMAN B.B. King
8 GET OUT OF MY LIFE, WOMAN Lee Dorsey
9 GO (BEFORE YOU BREAK MY HEART)
   Gigliola Cinquetti
10 GO AWAY FROM MY WORLD Marianne Faithfull ★

The above variations on a theme hopefully speak for themselves. An additional extreme parting shot, where the situation is desperate enough to warrant it, might be 'They're Coming To Take Me Away, Ha-Haaa!'

RECORDS THAT GO BUMP IN THE NIGHT . . . famous monsters of vinyl-land

1 THERE'S A GHOST IN MY HOUSE
   R. Dean Taylor
2 DINNER WITH DRAC John Zacherle
3 MONSTER MASH Bobby "Boris" Pickett
   & The Crypt-Kickers
4 DRACULA'S DAUGHTER Screaming Lord Sutch★
5 FRANKENSTEIN Edgar Winter
6 WEREWOLVES OF LONDON Warren Zevon
7 NIGHT OF THE VAMPIRE Moontrekkers
8 SPOOKY Classics IV
9 THE FANG Nervous Norvous
10 SHE'S IN LOVE WITH A MONSTER MAN Revillos
11 FEAST OF THE MAU MAU Screamin' Jay Hawkins
12 DR JECKYLL & MR HYDE Who
13 SEASON OF THE WITCH Donovan
14 HAUNTED HOUSE Gene Simmons
15 HAUNTED CASTLE Kingsmen
16 PURPLE PEOPLE EATER
   Sheb Woolley
17 THE SUPER-NATURAL
   John Mayall & Peter Green
18 PSYCHO KILLER
   Talking Heads
19 WEREWOLF Frantics
20 HUMAN FLY Cramps

Most of the above are purely for fun, of course, but for a record guaranteed to send a real cold chill down your spine, the compilers recommend a listen to James Brown's *King Heroin*. Brown was deadly serious when he made this harrowing anti-drug record; if it doesn't scare you, nothing will.

COLOUR ME POP

If you thought that most hit songs were about love or dancing or going places, roughly in that order, you would of course be correct. However, other categories crop up with remarkable regularity – songs about buildings and food (and not only by The Talking Heads), and a consistently remarkable number with a colour, or colours, as their theme.

We offer here a selection of brief but representative lists of variously-hued hits, old and not so old. Now, be honest; did you truly realise that colours like black and yellow were used quite so prolifically? It had not occurred to us until we started researching it.

A BLACK LIST

BLACK IS BLACK Los Bravos ★
PAINT IT BLACK Rolling Stones
BLACK BETTY Ram Jam
BLACK NIGHT Deep Purple
BLACK PEARL Sonny Charles
BLACK GIRL Four Pennies
BLACK AND WHITE Three Dog Night
THE REVEREND MR BLACK Kingston Trio
A WALK IN THE BLACK FOREST Horstz Jankowski
SAY IT LOUD – I'M BLACK AND I'M PROUD
  James Brown

TAKE IT AS RED

RED DRESS Alvin Stardust
RED RIVER ROCK Johnny & The Hurricanes
RED RED WINE Neil Diamond
RED BALLOON Dave Clark Five
ROSES ARE RED Bobby Vinton
RED SAILS IN THE SUNSET Fats Domino
RED LIGHT SPELLS DANGER Billy Ocean
LITTLE RED ROOSTER Sam Cooke
ROCKIN' RED WING Sammy Masters
SNOOPY VS THE RED BARON Royal Guardsmen

WHITER THAN WHITE

WHITE ON WHITE Danny Williams
WHITE BIRD It's A Beautiful Day
A WHITER SHADE OF PALE Procol Harum
WHITE ROOM Cream
WHITE RIOT Clash
WHITE PUNKS ON DOPE Tubes ★
WHITE CLIFFS OF DOVER Righteous Brothers
A WHITE SPORT COAT Marty Robbins
WHITE LIES Grin
WHITE LIGHTNIN' George Jones

GREEN AND BEAR IT

GREEN GREEN New Christy Minstrels
GREEN RIVER Creedence Clearwater Revival
GREEN ONIONS Booker T & The MGs
GREEN DOOR Shakin' Stevens
GREEN TAMBOURINE Lemon Pipers
GREEN GRASS Gary Lewis & The Playboys
GREEN EYED LADY Sugarloaf
GREENFIELDS Brothers Four
RHYTHM AND GREENS Shadows
GREEN GREEN GRASS OF HOME Tom Jones

WE BLUE IT

BLUE IS THE COLOUR Chelsea F.C.
I'M BLUE Ikettes
BLUE EYES Elton John ★
BLUE BAYOU Roy Orbison
BLUE GIRL Bruisers
BLUE MONDAY Fats Domino
BLUE BLUE DAY Don Gibson
BLUE ON BLUE Bobby Vinton
BLUE TURNS TO GREY Cliff Richard
BLUE MOON Marcels
BLUER THAN BLUE Rolf Harris

YELLOW PERILS

YELLOW PEARL Phil Lynott
MELLOW YELLOW Donovan
YELLOW RIVER Christie
BIG YELLOW TAXI Joni Mitchell ★
YELLOW SUBMARINE Beatles
18 YELLOW ROSES Bobby Darin
YELLOW ROSE OF TEXAS Mitch Miller
YELLOW BALLOON Jan And Dean
GOODBYE YELLOW BRICK ROAD Elton John
TIE A YELLOW RIBBON ROUND THE
  OLD OAK TREE Dawn

HUE DO YOU LOVE (other colours you *never* thought had been used for songs)

GOLD John Stewart ★
TURQUOISE Donovan
FADE TO GREY Visage
PURPLE HAZE Jimi Hendrix
SILVER MACHINE Hawkwind
ORANGE SKIES Love ★
OLD BROWN SHOE Beatles
PINK SHOE LACES Dodie Stevens
MOOD INDIGO Duke Ellington
COLOURS OF MY LOVE
    Jefferson (all right, we cheated!)

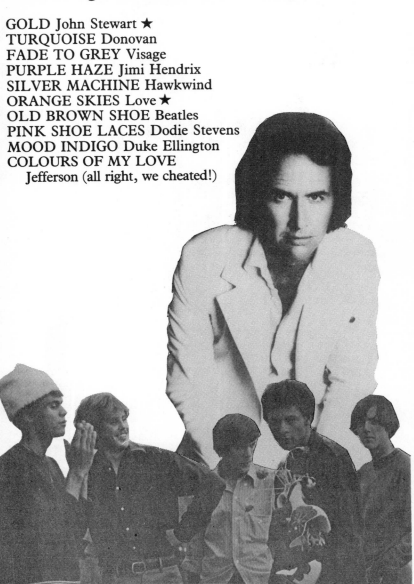

ODD BEHAVIOUR

I TALK TO THE TREES (Clint Eastwood)
CALLING OCCUPANTS OF INTERPLANETARY
   CRAFT (Carpenters) ★

I LOVE MY DOG (Cat Stevens)
YOU CAN'T ROLLER SKATE IN A BUFFALO HERD
   (Roger Miller)
I SOLD MY HEART TO THE JUNK MAN
   (Patti LaBelle & The Bluebells)
LOVING YOU HAS MADE ME BANANAS
   (Guy Marks)
I'M GONNA BE A WHEEL SOMEDAY (Fats Domino)
MAY THE BIRD OF PARADISE FLY UP YOUR NOSE
   (Little Jimmy Dickens)
I CAN'T GROW PEACHES ON A CHERRY TREE
   (Just Us)
I LOVE ONIONS (Susan Christie)

The world is full of strange people and, judging by the above, songwriters obviously constitute a reasonable proportion of them. We would
be glad to receive details of other certifiable occupations which have been
celebrated on popular vinyl like this.

LONDON TUBE STATIONS TOP TEN

BAKER STREET (Gerry Rafferty)
LONDON BRIDGE (Bread)
WATERLOO (Abba)
FINCHLEY CENTRAL (New Vaudeville Band)
VICTORIA (Kinks)
SUNNY GOODGE STREET (Donovan)
BOND STREET (Burt Bacharach)
ANGEL (Elvis Presley)
STRAIGHT TO THE BANK (Bill Summers)
DOWN IN THE TUBE STATION AT MIDNIGHT
    (Jam)

Whether you are familiar with London's Underground railway network
or not, you've got to look at the titles above and admit that this list is
pretty damn clever. We're glad we didn't try to make it a top 20, however.

ALCOHOLIC DRINKS TOP TEN

SHERRY (Four Seasons)
BRANDY (Scott English)
WHISKY IN THE JAR (Thin Lizzy)
GIN HOUSE (Amen Corner)
RED RED WINE (Neil Diamond)
A PUB WITH NO BEER (Slim Dusty)
TEQUILA (Champs)
ONE MINT JULEP (Ray Charles)
GLASS OF CHAMPAGNE (Sailor)
I AM A CIDER DRINKER (Wurzels)

NON-ALCOHOLIC DRINKS TOP TEN

FROZEN ORANGE JUICE
(Peter Sarstedt) ★
THE COFFEE SONG
(Frank Sinatra)
NO MILK TODAY
(Herman's Hermits)
WATER, WATER
(Tommy Steele)
TEA FOR TWO CHA CHA
(Tommy Dorsey Orchestra)
HOT CHOCOLATE CRAZY
(Eden Kane)
SIPPIN' SODA
(Guy Mitchell)
MILKSHAKE MADAMOISELLE
(Jerry Lee Lewis)
CHINA TEA
(Russ Conway)
40 CUPS OF COFFEE
(Bill Haley & The Comets)

These, of course, are selective lists, but it is noticeable that the alcoholic drinks, with two million-sellers in their ranks, generally seem to inspire more hit records. All right and proper, since booze and rock'n'roll have always gone hand in hand. The first reader to write in to complain that 'Sherry' and 'Brandy' are actually supposed to be girls' names will qualify for the compilers' Pub Bore of the Year award.

SOME MORE VERY LONG AND SILLY SONG TITLES

We chose the *crème de la crème* of these for our first volume in this series, and somewhat to our surprise they were by far the most popular and heavily quoted amongst the reviewing and broadcasting fraternity. Indeed, we found ourselves reciting the title of Fairport Convention's "Sir B McKenzie's Daughter's Lament etc., etc., etc." over the nation's airwaves on more than one occasion.

We make no apologies for this second "long and silly" list failing to scale the heights attained by its predecessor. We can, however, offer you enough lengthy and loony song titles to still make you question the sanity of some of the songwriting fraternity . . .

MISS PAMELA AND MISS SPARKY DISCUSS STUFFED BRAS AND SOME OF THEIR EARLY GYM CLASS EXPERIENCES The GTOs ★

A SMALL PACKAGE OF VALUE WILL COME TO YOU, SHORTLY Jefferson Airplane

THE WALTZ THAT CARRIED US AWAY AND THEN A MOSQUITO CAME AND ATE UP MY SWEETHEART John Fahey ★

PRELUDE TO THE AFTERNOON
OF A SEXUALLY AROUSED GAS
MASK Frank Zappa ★

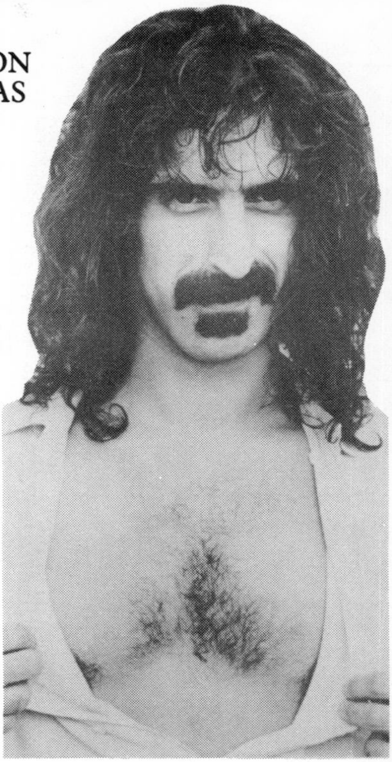

DO ME IN ONCE AND I'LL BE
SAD, DO ME IN TWICE AND
I'LL KNOW BETTER
Circular Circulation

MAYBE THE PEOPLE WOULD
BE THE TIMES OR BETWEEN
CLARKE AND HILLDALE
Love

IF I COULD DO IT ALL OVER
AGAIN, I'D DO IT ALL OVER
YOU
Caravan

YOU GET MORE FOR
YOUR MONEY ON THE
FLIPSIDE OF THE RECORD
TALKING BLUES
Kim Fowley

(THE STRANGE
 CIRCUMSTANCES
 WHICH LED TO)
VLADIMIR AND OLGA
(REQUESTING
 REHABILITATION
 IN A SIBERIAN HEALTH
 RESORT AS A RESULT OF STRESS IN
FURTHERING THE PEOPLE'S POLICIES)
Stranglers

And one album title which we felt we had to include here because it is not
only long but also *extremely* silly:

SEE JUNGLE! SEE JUNGLE! GO JOIN YOUR GANG,
   YEAH, CITY ALL OVER! GO APE CRAZY!
Bow Wow Wow

Printed in Great Britain